BEFORE THE CURSE

ALSO BY TROY SOOS

BEFORE THE CURSE

THE GLORY DAYS OF
NEW ENGLAND BASEBALL: 1858–1918

TROY SOOS

PARNASSUS IMPRINTS
Hyannis, Massachusetts

First Edition

Parnassus Imprints
30 Perseverance Way
Hyannis, MA 02601

Library of Congress Catalog Number: 97-65476

Manufactured in the United States of America

For Gretel, who survived the Little League years

ACKNOWLEDGEMENTS

A number of people contributed to this book in different ways, and I am grateful for all their assistance and encouragement.

I'd especially like to thank my editor, Wallace Exman, for his enthusiasm and guidance; Justine Klein, for her work on the layout of the book; and my agents, Meredith Bernstein and Elizabeth Cavanaugh, for their continuing efforts on my behalf.

Many members of the Society for American Baseball Research (SABR) generously shared the fruits of their own research with me. Particularly helpful were Seamus Kearney, on town ball and the Twin State League; Jerry Malloy, on early black baseball; Mark Rucker of Transcendental Graphics, who located and documented many of the photographs; and Tom Simon, on the Northern League. Also providing valuable information and assistance were: Will Anderson, Phil Bergen, Merritt Clifton, Elias Dudash, Michael Gershman (who also provided photos from the Gavin Riley collection), Dennis Goldstein, Barry Halper, Fred Ivor-Campbell, Laura Kelly, Len Levin, Karl Lindholm, Lew Lipset, Joe Overfield, Nat Rosenberg, Tom Shieber, John Thorn, and Bob Wood.

Librarians, archivists, and researchers from institutions throughout the region helped in tracking down photographs and documents. My thanks go to: Harold Barry, Brattleboro Historical Society; Jean Berry and Wilma Slaight, Wellesley College Archives; Julie Bressor, Mack Librarian for Special Collections at Norwich University; Sylvia Kennick Brown, Archives and Special Collections of Williams College; W. C. Burdick, the National Baseball Library & Archive; Peter Carini, Mount Holyoke College Archives; Daria D'Arienzo, Amherst College Library; Joanne Dougherty, Smith College Archives; Madeline Gifford, Bangor Historical Society; Danielle Green, Harvard University Archives; Barbara L. Krieger, Dartmouth College Library; Jennifer MacKenzie, The Gunnery School Library; William Massa, Yale University Library Manuscripts and Archives; Richard McBride, Meriden Public Library; Mary McMullen, New Haven Register; Janet T. Murphy, The Connecticut Historical Society; Leroy Rand, Maine Baseball Hall of Fame; Susan Raudin, Bowdoin College Special Collections Library; Elias Rodriguez, Sports Illustrated Library; Mark Savolis, Holy Cross College Archives; Aaron Schmidt, Print Department of the Boston Public Library; Brad Sullivan, SABR Lending Library; Jamelle Tanous, Fall River Historical Society; Peter Tomlinson, Culver Pictures; John Whiting, Enosburg Falls Historical Society. Extensive assistance was provided by Jessie Rabban, Martha Hamilton and Norman Waksler, of the Cambridge Public Library, and by the staff of the Microtext Room of the Boston Public Library.

I deeply appreciate the efforts made by others to provide information that is as accurate as can be determined. Any errors that may be found in the book are mine, not theirs.

CONTENTS

PREFACE

The years following 1918—the last time that the Boston Red Sox won a World Series—have been filled with raised expectations, dashed hopes, and continuing frustration for New England baseball fans. The decades of suffering after "The Curse" fell upon the Sox are known all too well.

But what about before The Curse? That era, the period before World War I, is the most colorful one in baseball history, and the subject of this book.

New England baseball has a remarkably rich heritage, extending far beyond Boston and the Red Sox. The region was home of the first World's Champions, the 1884 Providence Grays, and the scene of the first intercollegiate baseball game, played by Amherst and Williams in Pittsfield in 1859. Baseball's first major league included three Connecticut franchises: Hartford, Middletown, and New Haven. Major league baseball's first perfect game was hurled in 1880 by a Brown University student who pitched part-time for the National League Worcester Brown Stockings.

In the nineteenth century, there were strong major-league teams in Boston, Hartford, Providence, and Worcester. New England colleges—Bowdoin, Brown, Dartmouth, Harvard, and Yale—fielded teams that often beat the professionals. Minor leagues flourished; the New England League was one of the finest in the country; and there were local leagues in every state—the Connecticut League, the Rhode Island League, the Maine State League, and the Twin States (Vermont and New Hampshire) League. There were mill leagues and town clubs and barnstorming teams like the Boston Bloomer Girls and the Providence Independents. Black baseball was represented by the Boston Resolutes, the Chelsea Auroras, and the Commonwealth Giants. From mill towns to seaports, from villages to cities, New Englanders were playing baseball.

To help present as vivid a picture as possible of early New England baseball—the game, the players, the cities, and the times—this book includes dozens of archival photographs and accounts of historic games taken from contemporary sources. Newspaper reports have been edited for length but not for content; players' names are often misspelled, box score totals do not always add up, and there are some spectacular run-on sentences.

My hope is that *Before the Curse* will provide a sense of what baseball was like when the game was taking hold as the National Pastime and New England was playing a vital role in its growth.

Troy Soos
Cambridge, Massachusetts
January 1997

THE EARLY YEARS:
From Children's Game to Gentlemen's Pastime

At the dawn of the nineteenth century, a dozen various games involving balls, bats, and bases were being played by boys and girls on village greens, city schoolyards, and rural pastures. Within a few decades, elements of these games were incorporated into a new sport called "base ball."

The most rapid evolution of the game occurred during the period from the 1840s through the 1860s, as grown men took up what had once been strictly a children's pursuit and gave it an adult structure and formality. They organized clubs, then associations of clubs. State and regional tournaments were held, with teams playing for prizes of silver baseballs and golden bats. Rules were codified and disseminated through annual playing guides such as *Beadle's Dime Base-Ball Player* and *DeWitt's Base Ball Guide*. Weekly sporting papers—*Wilkes' Spirit of the Times,* the *New York Clipper,* the *New England Base Ballist*—reported on matches and players and helped popularize the game.

By 1869, professional ballplayers were performing before thousands of paying spectators, and baseball was already being referred to as "the National Pastime."

GAMES OF BALL

The children of America's earliest settlers brought with them the recreations of their old countries, including a number of games of ball. In early New England, although the Puritans discouraged such leisure activities (the governor of Plymouth Colony went so far as to issue a ban on ball playing), these games continued and new ones were devised.

Among the ball games that boys and girls played were "goal ball," "base," "feeder," "soak ball," "stool ball" (in which milking stools were used as bases), and "barn ball." Barn ball was a simple, two-player game that contained some of the basic elements of baseball: one player threw a ball against a barn and the second player struck the rebounding ball with a bat; the batsman then raced to touch the barn wall and return "home" before the opposing player could field the ball and hit him with it. If the batter made it safely, he scored; if he was struck with the ball, he was out, and the other player went to bat for his "inning."

Boys playing an early form of baseball on Boston Common (the State House is in the background.) This woodcut appeared in *The Book of Sports* by Robin Carver, published in Boston in 1834. Although the illustration shows a game indistinguishable from rounders, the rules of play that Carver gives are headed "Base, or Goal Ball."

The games "one-old-cat," "two-old-cat," "three-old-cat," and "four-old-cat" dispensed with the barn and permitted additional boys to play. "Cat" was short for "catapult," referring to the bat. Four-old-cat, the most elaborate of this kind of ball game, required eight players: four bases were laid out in a square, and a fielder and a batter were stationed at each base. As the fielders threw the ball from one base to another, the batters attempted to hit it and run to the next base. Each player scored only for himself, not as part of a team. The unwieldiness of four-old-cat (as well as, perhaps, the inevitable conflicts that must have resulted with four boys brandishing bats at the same time) proved a limit to its appeal.

The most popular game of ball, and the most direct forerunner of baseball, was the old English game of "rounders." Rounders, which was played by girls as well as boys, was a team sport. The playing field consisted of four bases, usually in a diamond pattern. The ball was small and soft; the bat was the size of a policeman's billy club. The "feeder" of the team in the field would throw the ball to the "striker" of the team at bat. If the striker succeeded in hitting the ball, the "scouts" attempted to field it and "soak" the batter by hitting him with the ball when he was between bases. Rounders and early baseball were so similar that in some cases rules for the game printed in British books were reprinted by American publishers with no change except for the name of the game: Base Ball.

THE MASSACHUSETTS GAME

In the 1830s, men seeking outdoor exercise started to take up the ball games of their boyhoods. It would have been "unmanly" for them to play rounders, since that was a game for girls and boys, so they called their sport "base ball" or "town ball." Although the name was different, the game they played was virtually identical to the one that they had played as children. (The attempt to distance baseball from its rounders origin continued for decades, eventually leading to the creation of the Abner Doubleday myth.)

For some years, there were no set rules to town ball, and playing rules were agreed to on a match-by-match basis. Eventually, regional variations of the game evolved. In the Philadelphia area, five bases were used. New England town ball was played on a square field, with no fixed number of players to a team. In 1845, New York's Knickerbocker Base Ball Club established rules that became the basis for "modern" baseball: the practice of hitting runners with the ball was eliminated, only balls hit between first and third bases were in play, and three outs ended a team's inning at bat. In the 1850s, two forms of baseball vied for dominance: the "New York Game" and the "Massachusetts Game."

The first organized ball club in New England was the 1854 Olympic Club of Boston, soon followed by the Elm Trees, the Green Mountains, and the Takewambaits. These clubs all played the Massachusetts Game.

There were several aspects of the Massachusetts Game that limited its appeal. One was the practice of putting runners out by "soaking" them with the ball. Another was the fact that *every* batted ball was in play; this led to a batting strategy of letting the ball tick off the bat to fly over the head of the catcher—while effective, it made for a play

Right: The diagram of the ball field included in *The Rules of the Massachusetts Game* shows the square layout used in town ball. The bases were four-foot high wooden stakes. There were no foul lines since any "struck" ball, no matter how slightly tipped or in what direction it traveled, was in play. The "thrower" was only thirty-five feet from the "striker." Other than the thrower and catcher, fielding positions were not designated; there was no need to cover particular bases since there were no force plays—a runner not in contact with a base was put out by "plugging" or "soaking" him with a thrown ball.

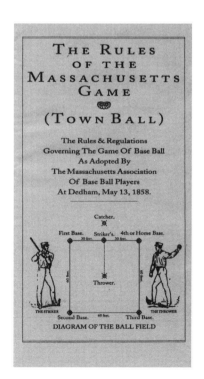

This image, simply titled "Base Ball Club," is from a set of stereoviews published in Boston circa 1865. The photograph, possibly taken as early as 1859, depicts game action on Boston Common, with Beacon Street houses in the background. According to historian Mark Rucker, this is the only known photograph of the Massachusetts style game in progress. *Photo courtesy of Transcendental Graphics*

that was less than scintillating. Finally, matches continued until one team had scored 100 "tallies," leading to some interminable contests (on October 11, 1859, the Excelsiors of Upton and the Medway Unions played for 11 hours over the course of two days, until Upton came away with a 100–56 victory).

The first challenge to the traditional New England style of play came when the Boston Tri-Mountain Club organized in 1857. The Tri-Mountains (named for the three hills that were once part of Boston's topography) adopted the New York Game and urged other clubs to play according to its rules as well. Resistance was strong. On May 13, 1858, representatives of ten clubs convened in Dedham, Massachusetts. They formed the Massachusetts Association of Base Ball Players, and codified town ball playing rules. The Tri-Mountain Club vigorously advocated the new style of baseball, and when the other members of the Association insisted that only the "Massachusetts Game" be played, the Tri-Mountains quit the Association.

Undaunted, the Tri-Mountains continued to champion the new game and eventually won a number of converts. After their historic 1858 match against Portland on Boston Common, teams throughout New England abandoned Town Ball for the New York Game.

Although some traditionalists persisted (the Massachusetts Association of Base Ball Players met again on April 7, 1860 to revise the rules and change their name to the New England Association of Base Ball Players), by the end of the 1860s, the Massachusetts Game had virtually vanished.

SEPT. 9, 1858: AN INTERESTING GAME OF BASE BALL

The Boston Tri-Mountains Club organized in 1857 with the intent of playing the "New York" style of baseball. They faced one major obstacle: no team in the area would play them according to those rules. Finally, after a year of practicing only among themselves, the Tri-Mountains found a willing opponent. The Portland Club traveled from Maine to face the Tri-Mountains in a match on Boston Common.

The game was played on September 9, 1858, and the new style of play attracted considerable attention, including that of a *Boston Herald* reporter. The day after the match, in the same column as items titled "Dead Body Found" and "Rogues Caught," the *Herald* ran the following piece:

An Interesting Game of Base Ball on the Common— The Portland Club of Portland, Me., vs. the Tri-Mountain Club of Boston.

A very closely contested game of base ball was played on the Common in this city yesterday afternoon, between the Portland Club of Portland, Me., and the Tri-Mountain Club of Boston. The game was that known as the New York game, and the Portland boys won by five runs. The rules of the New York game differ materially from those adopted by the Massachusetts Association of Base Ball Players last fall. The bases are placed at the angles of a rhombus instead of a square, the home base being the position of the striker; provision is made for "foul hits," and the ball is caught on the "bound" as well as on the "fly." The game consists of nine innings instead of one hundred tallies, and the ball is pitched, not thrown.

The playing commenced about three o'clock, the Tri-Mountain Club having the first innings, and the ninth innings of the Portland Club was finished at a quarter to six. Mr. J. E. Burt of the Tri-Mountain Club had one of his hands badly injured in the first innings by a blow from the ball, and his place was filled during the remainder of the game by Mr. Henry F. Gill. Mr. Crowell of the Portland Club was severely affected by the heat, and was obliged to give up for a time, but he soon recovered and resumed playing. His place was filled by Mr. Childs, another member of the Club, during one or two innings. The playing was witnessed by a large and interested crowd of spectators. The following is the score of the game:—

TRI-MOUNTAIN CLUB	H. L.	Runs		PORTLAND CLUB	H. L.	Runs
G. E. Guild, catcher	1	7		E. N. Robinson, catcher	6	4
H. F. Gill, 3d base	3	6		S. M. Eaton, pitcher	3	5
C. C. Dimon, 1st base	1	5		S. Crowell, 2d base	3	5
G. F. Goldthwait, 2d base	5	0		J. C. M. Furbish, r. field	4	5

F. N. Scott, c. field	1	4		G. H. Abbott, l. field	2	6
G. Troupe, r. field	5	4		J. B. Winslow, 3d base	2	5
G. Arnold, Jr., l. field	4	5		G. M. Woodbury, 1st base	4	5
W. H. Bourne, short	5	4		Samuel Chadwick, short	2	7
I. H. Ware, pitcher	2	7		J. M. Knight, c. field	1	5
Total		42		Total		47

RUNS MADE IN EACH INNINGS

	1st	2d	3d	4th	5th	6th	7th	8th	9th	Total
Tri-Mountain	0	5	0	11	13	1	0	7	1	42
Portland	2	0	2	7	9	4	5	10	8	47

Number of balls pitched by Ware, of the Tri-Mountain Club, 143; passed Guild, the catcher, 5; caught on the fly, 2. Number pitched by Eaton, of the Portland Club, 115; passed Robinson, the catcher, 4; caught on the fly, 4.

Umpire—Richard Tower of the Tri-Mountain Club. Scorers—A. P. Margott of the Tri-Mountain Club and C. G. Gammon of the Portland Club.

(Box score note: "H.L." stands for "Hands Lost," roughly the equivalent of "Outs.")

A GENTLEMEN'S SPORT

Baseball clubs of the 1850s and 1860s often bore a greater resemblance to social clubs and fraternal orders than to athletic teams. For many of these gentlemen's clubs, ball games were almost incidental; the rituals that surrounded them were what mattered, not the scores. Challenges to other clubs were presented as formal invitations, the progressions to the playing grounds often took the form of parades with each club bringing an entourage of supporters, and, most importantly, there were extravagant post-game dinners featuring loquacious toasts and speeches. Published game accounts often included descriptions of the carriages used to transport the teams, the dress of the onlookers, and the menus of the banquets that followed the matches.

During the actual matches, good sportsmanship and gentlemanly conduct were considered of paramount importance. Although rules of the time stipulated that a batter was out if a batted ball was caught on the first "bound," fielders were expected to attempt to catch the ball on the fly because it was considered more manly. In 1865 the rule was changed, specifying that a batter was only out if the ball was caught before it touched the ground. In addition to exhibiting "good form" in their play, club members had to observe decorum on the field—fines were assessed on the spot for incidents of swearing, disobedience to the team captain, expressing an opinion on the outcome of a play before the umpire gave his decision, or disputing the umpire's call.

To the

LOWELL B. B. CLUB

BOSTON.

The Match Committee of the

WAMSUTTA

BASE BALL CLUB

OF NEW BEDFORD,

HEREBY CHALLENGE your First Nine to play a Match Game of Ball at New Bedford, at your earliest convenience.

C. W. Clifford

S. Van Campen Committee

N. E. Howland

New Bedford Oct 9th 1868

An elaborately penned invitation, dated Oct. 9, 1868, from the Wamsutta Base Ball Club of New Bedford challenging the "first nine" of the Boston Lowells to a match "at your earliest convenience." It is difficult to understand why the Wamsuttas were so eager for a rematch, since only two months earlier they'd been drubbed by the Lowells by a score of 62 to 6 in seven innings. *Photo courtesy of the Boston Public Library, Print Department.*

Above: The 1866 Boston Lowells. Originally organized as a junior club in 1861, the team adopted its name in honor of John Lowell, catcher with the Boston Bowdoins, who encouraged the young players and supplied them with equipment. The Lowells soon established themselves as New England's dominant team of the 1860's, once defeating the Flyaways of East Boston by a score of 121–14. Popular star James D'Wolf Lovett is pictured fourth from left in the photograph. Proudly displayed in the box on the table is the Silver Ball representing the Championship of New England. *Photo courtesy of Transcendental Graphics.*

A number of clubs did pay more attention to athletics than dining, however, and established strong and skillful teams. Most were in Massachusetts: the King Philip Club of Abington, the Eurekas of East Cambridge, the Fitchburg Rollstones, Framingham's Pickwick Club, the Granite Club of Holliston, Lowell Clippers, Marlboro Fairmounts, Natick Eagles, Pittsfield Old Elms, Quincy Actives, Springfield Pioneers, Taunton Metacomets, and Worcester Excelsiors; Boston teams included the Beacons, Bowdoins, Fly Aways, Lowells, and Tri-Mountains. Providence had several first-rate teams including the Blackstones, Juniors, and Olympics. In Maine, the Augusta Cushnocs, Norway Pennessewassees, and Portland Eons were dominant. Connecticut's leading clubs were the Hartford Charter Oaks, Norwalk Libertys, Stratford Osceolas, and Waterburys. There were few early teams in New Hampshire or Vermont; of them, the Rockingham Club of Portsmouth, New Hampshire, was the best known and the strongest.

So many teams were springing up throughout New England, that eight years after changing its name from the Massachusetts Association of Base Ball Players to the New England Association of Base Ball Players, the organization reverted to a state association. Other states, which now had enough clubs to form their own associations, organized local leagues and tournaments. In the Rhode Island Championship of 1868 the Providence Olympics beat the Burrillville Wide Awakes by a score of 78–20. That same year, Maine had tournaments for both senior and junior divisions; the Eons defeated the Cushnocs to take the senior title and a silver ball, and the Augusta Dirigos outplayed the Portland Rising Stars to win the junior championship and a "gold mounted bat." With the focus on winning, baseball became more competitive and less genteel. Good form was relegated to lesser importance than aggressive play and successful results. Rivalries, not always friendly, developed between teams and cities. Tournaments were organized, and clubs assigned their members into "first nines," "second nines," and sometimes "third nines" according to skill level. Junior clubs of younger players were established and occasionally functioned as farm systems for the men's teams.

Not even the devastation of war could slow the game's progress. The immediate impact of the Civil War on gentlemen's ball clubs, especially in New England, was minimal. While some players left their teams for military service, others remained on the playing field instead of the battlefield. A drafted man was allowed an exemption from serving either by paying a fee of $300 or by hiring a substitute to fight in his place. The affluent men who made up gentlemen's clubs were easily able to afford these exemptions.

During the four years of war, baseball was actually spread by soldiers who played it in camps and forts. At the end of the conflict, they brought the game home with them and organized their own teams and leagues. Baseball was soon taken up by every social class. The gentlemen's clubs lost their dominance, and the game was being played by farmers, mill hands, firemen, and machinists.

ON CAMPUS

College students, almost entirely males in their teens and early twenties, were of such an age that they were able to enjoy baseball both as boyish recreation and as structured

Rockingham Nine of Portsmouth, New Hampshire, ca. 1867. This photograph provides a rare view of the circular iron plates that served as home base and the pitcher's point during this era. Circular plates were obsolete by 1869, but the terms "plate" and "dish" have remained part of baseball's vocabulary. *Photo courtesy of Transcendental Graphics.*

social activity. Throughout the first century of baseball's evolution, the game flourished on New England campuses.

There are surprisingly early references to college ball games. Daniel Webster wrote that he spent his free time "playing at ball" while a Dartmouth undergraduate in the 1790s. Oliver Wendell Holmes remembered playing ball at Harvard in the 1820s. As a student at Bowdoin College in 1824, Henry Wadsworth Longfellow reported, "there is nothing now heard of, in our leisure hours, but ball, ball, ball. I cannot prophesy with any degree of accuracy concerning the continuance of this rage for play, but the effect is good, since there has been a throroughgoing reformation from inactivity and torpitude."

Initially, the college games were casual affairs, with no fixed rosters or schedules. Teams then started to be organized by class. The first documented baseball game in Maine took place on October 10, 1860 between the senior class team of Bowdoin College and the Sunrise Club of Brunswick. In 1862, the Boston Lowells helped establish the first club at Harvard, which was made up of the freshmen class of 1866. Class nines at Yale were organized in 1865.

Soon after class teams were established, the best players of the teams were selected for "university nines" to represent their schools. Within a few years, colleges throughout New England—Amherst, Bowdoin, Brown, Dartmouth, Harvard, Middlebury, Tufts, Wesleyan, Williams, Yale—had active baseball programs.

July 1, 1859: Base Ball and Chess! Muscle and Mind!!

In the spring of 1859, the students of Amherst College challenged Williams College to a game of baseball. Williams accepted, but countered Amherst with a challenge to a chess match (a game at which Williams excelled) so that there might be "a trial of mind as well as muscle." Thus the first intercollegiate game in baseball history was played as part of a baseball-chess "double header."

The Base-Ball Club of Pittsfield offered the use of their grounds, a field "well adapted to the long, front-and-back play of the Massachusetts game." Each college supplied its own ball: the Amherst ball was "a work of art" made by Henry Hebard of North Brookfield; the Williams ball, slightly larger, was "covered with leather of some light color, drab or buff, so as not to be easily distinguished by the batter."

Since neither college had an organized baseball club, teams were chosen by ballot from the student bodies of each school (the Amherst thrower, however, was rumored to be a professional blacksmith). The teams agreed to play according to modified rules of the Massachusetts Game, with 13 players on a side, and a total of 65 tallies needed to win the match.

On July 1, the teams met in Pittsfield, on grounds "north of the Town lot, and east of the Maplewood Institute." They played 26 innings with one recess. An *Extra* broadside of the *Amherst Express* reported the outcome (in language which makes evident the differences between the Massachusetts Game and modern baseball):

**WILLIAMS AND AMHERST
BASE BALL AND CHESS!
<u>MUSCLE AND MIND!!</u>**
AMHERST WINS!
Amherst 73. Williams 32.

Amherst certainly played the better, in nearly every department of the game. In knocking they had the advantage of side-strikes and back-knocks—in running, Williams certainly excelled as far as speed is concerned, but lost at least eight or ten innings, by premature efforts, while the Amherst players ran only at the word of the captain—in fielding, Williams made equally good catches; but in passing in, they threw too wildly, each where he pleased, and nothing is more injurious than bad out-play.

More than all, Amherst took the lead by its perfect, military discipline. All was done with the accuracy of clock work. The Amherst captain governed his men with great skill. There were not a half a dozen bad plays, on that side, in the course of the game.

The game closed at 2 1/2 o'clock, having lasted 3 1/2 hours. A large and excited company of ladies and gentlemen from the place watched the whole progress of the game, and cheered the players by their presence as well as by loud applause and the waving of signals. The beauty of Pittsfield was gathered to grace and honor the chivalry of the two colleges.

SCORE:

AMHERST CLUB			WILLIAMS CLUB		
Players	*Tallies*	*Outs*	*Players*	*Tallies*	*Outs*
Claflin, catcher	7	0	*Parker*	0	4
Pierce	5	2	*Fitch*	0	5
Storrs	7	1	*Blagden*	1	5
Tower	7	1	*Simmons*	4	1
Cushman	4	3	*Brown,*	3	3
Evans	5	4	*Hastings*	4	1
Fenn	5	0	*Quick*	3	1
Hyde, thrower	4	3	*Pratt*	2	2
Leach	6	0	*Knox*	4	0
Roome	5	4	*Bush*	4	1
Gridley	5	4	*Beecher, thrower*	3	2
Pratt	7	2	*Nichols*	2	0
Tomson	6	2	*Anderson, catcher*	2	1
Total	73			32	

Thus has ended a match, which has brought with it many incidents not soon to be forgotten.

The students of Amherst rejoice not merely in the fact, that in this contest their Alma Mater has borne away the laurels; but also in the belief that by such encounters as these, a deeper interest will be excited in those amusements, which, while they serve as a relaxation from study, strengthen and develop body and mind.

The day after the baseball game, Amherst upset favored Williams at chess, completing its sweep of the "muscle and mind" double header.

Since the universities were considered training grounds for young gentlemen, it was natural that the established gentlemen's baseball clubs helped foster the sport among students. Some rivalries—initially friendly—developed between the college teams and local adult clubs. Among them were Bowdoin and the Sunrise Club, Harvard and the Lowells, and Yale and the Hartford Charter Oaks.

Without any structured athletic conferences or intercollegiate schedules, many of the university nines played most of their matches against men's teams instead of against other colleges. The students took on the best clubs in baseball, and often beat them. By the end of the 1860's, the college teams themselves were among the strongest in the country.

Above: During its 1859 game with Amherst, the only thing uniform about the Williams College attire was a team belt with "Williams" imprinted on the back (a step up from the Amherst players, who were described as "decidedly in undress"). Shown here is the 1865 Williams team, still lacking suitable uniforms. The year before this photograph was taken, on July 29, 1864, Williams and Harvard played a highly-publicized match in Worcester. With the winning run scoring on a steal of home, underdog Williams upset the Harvard team, which had never before lost a game in college play. *Photo courtesy of the Williams College Archives and Special Collections.*

Above: In uniforms apparently modeled after those worn during the recent Civil War, the 1866 Dartmouth College baseball team sits for its portrait. A student reported on the team's successful season in a letter dated Sept. 28, 1866: "The Dartmouth base ball club have been twice challenged by the Kearsarge base ball club of Concord—& came off victorious in both games. The first was played here. The second game was played yesterday at Concord & as the Concord club had previously beaten the Portsmouth club—& these three are the only ones in the State—one of the newspapers speaks of the Dartmouth club as 'the State Champions.'" *Photo courtesy of the Dartmouth College Library.*

June 17, 1868: A Trifle Disconcerted by the Sharp Fielding of Brown

In June of 1868, the Boston Lowells undertook a road trip through New England, defeating every club they faced. On June 17, the tour concluded in Rhode Island with a game against Brown University. Expecting an easy victory, a large contingent of Boston fans traveled to Providence to celebrate what Lowell's pitcher James Lovett called "the apotheosis." The day of the game, the *Providence Journal* sounded pessimistic about Brown's chances against the powerful Boston team:

> There will be a match game of base ball played on the Dexter Training Ground, this afternoon, at 2 o'clock, between the Lowell Club of Boston and the Sophomore nine of Brown University. The Lowells claim to be, and doubtless are, the champion club of New England, they having beaten, during their recent tour through the New England states, the Yale University nine, the Charter Oaks of Hartford, and several other more or less noted baseball organizations. The regular Brown nine are in a somewhat broken up condition, owing to the absence of several of their principal players, and the Sophomore nine have therefore accepted the challenge. We may anticipate an interesting game.

What transpired was one of the greatest upsets of the era. The *Journal* reported the following day:

BROWN VICTORIOUS

> A very interesting and closely contested match game of base ball was played on Dexter Training Ground, Wednesday afternoon, between the Sophomore nine of Brown University, and the Lowell Club of Boston. The game was called at about half-past two, and continued until about half-past five, without intermission. At the close of the ninth innings the score stood, Brown, 22, Lowell, 19, and Brown was therefore declared the winner by three runs. This announcement was received with vociferous cheering by the immense crowd which had congregated to witness the game. The Lowells returned to the City Hotel in carriages, while the students formed in line, and escorted their successful comrades to the college campus. The playing on both sides was particularly fine, especially between the pitcher and first and second bases of Brown, which was very sharp, and elicited considerable applause. Handsome fly catches were made Messrs. Monroe, Colwell, Taylor and Bowker, of the Brown nine, and by Messrs. Lovett, Bradbury, Newton and Rogers, of the Lowells. The Lowells won the toss for first innings, and went to bat, but were a trifle disconcerted by the sharp fielding of Brown, and lost the first two innings without scoring a single run. From the start Brown led, at the close of the sixth innings the score standing exactly two to one in their favor, and winding up with a majority of three, as already stated. We append the score of the game:

SOPHOMORE NINE	Outs	Runs	LOWELL CLUB	Outs	Runs
Monroe, c	3	3	Lovett, p.	4	3
Taylor, 1st b.	4	2	Joslin, 3d b.	3	2
Mattison, l. f.	1	5	Rogers, c. f.	4	2
Bowker, 2d b.	0	6	Sumner, 2d b.	2	3
Fales, 1st b.	1	4	Jewell, 1st b.	3	2
Grant, s. s.	5	0	Alline, r. f.	4	1
Hitchcock, r. f.	3	1	Bradbury, c.	2	2
Herreshoff, p	6	0	Newton, l. f.	2	2
Colwell, c. f.	4	1	Wilder, s. s.	3	2
Total	27	22	Total	27	19

(Note: the published box score shows two first basemen for Brown.)

Mr. John A. Lowell, of Boston, a member of the Lowell club, acted as umpire on the occassion, and discharged the duties of that office with signal ability, and in a manner entirely free from any appearance of partiality.

To commemorate their astonishing victory, the Brown team held a reunion every five years on the anniversary of the great game, a tradition which continued for fifty years.

SILVER BALL CHAMPIONSHIP

In 1864, John A. Lowell, founder of the engraving business of Lowell and Brett, commissioned a silver baseball to be awarded for the Championship of New England. Lowell was one of the most prominent figures of baseball's early years. In 1868, the *New England Base Ballist* said of him, "There is doubtless no person connected with our New England Base Ball Clubs more widely known, or held in higher esteem among the fraternity," and that, "from his efforts in advancing the interests of our National Game in this section of the country much of its success is due." Lowell had been president of the Boston Bowdoin Club, patron to the fledgling Lowell Club, and a highly respected and sought-after umpire.

The first match for possession of the Silver Ball was played between Boston's Tri-Mountains and the Osceolas of Portland, a game won by the Tri-Mountains 53–18. They held the trophy for only a week before losing it to the Boston Lowells.

Competition for the trophy generated tremendous enthusiasm among players and fans alike. Matches were played before thousands of cheering spectators while bands played the *Silver Ball March*. The results of each championship game were engraved on the ball before its presentation to the victor. Only three teams, the three New England powerhouses, ever held the Silver Ball: the Lowells, the Tri-Mountains, and Harvard.

Aug. 19, 1868: A Most Exciting Muffin Match

In addition to a club's "first nine" (their strongest lineup) and "second nine," many had a "muffin nine" comprised of their most inept players. Club members (especially those on the first or second nines) delighted in watching these muffins (they "muffed" plays) stumble about the field, and a "muffin match" was considered great entertainment. The *New England Base Ballist* of Aug. 20, 1868 reported on one such game:

MUFFIN GAME
WOODBURY VS. SUMNER

The most exciting muffin match of the season took place yesterday afternoon on the Common. Both nines were selected with great care from some of the best muffins in the business, and were all in sound condition when the game commenced, but some were slightly injured, our friend Woodbury for instance, when trying to soar for a fly, caught it on his finger nail, causing him to see stars, also much physical anguish; the game resulted in a victory for Sumner's side by a score of 55 to 35—uneven innings—G. D. W. Lovett, umpire—E. C. Nichols, scorer. After the game was called, on account of the darkness, the entire party adjourned to Blane's French Restaurant, and partook of a fine dinner. Mr. Woodbury made some pleasing remarks in presenting Mr. A. Rice with a large wax doll for making the poorest score—two other prizes were given out, including the muffin bats which Mssrs. Sumner and Woodbury have had the honor of holding. After some fine singing, speeches, & c., the party left for their homes, much pleased with the day's doings.

For three years, the Silver Ball was the most coveted prize among New England baseball clubs. Then it was withdrawn from circulation. Squabbling over the trophy had tarnished its image, as well as that of the amateur game. Teams that held the ball tried to avoid playing matches that might result in their having to relinquish it. Teams that failed to win the trophy wanted individual medals made from the silver so that every ball club could have at least a small prize. An intense feud developed between Harvard and the Lowells, with the formerly friendly rivals arguing over the dates and locations of Silver Ball contests, and each trying to arrange the scheduling to its own advantage; fans took up sides between the two clubs and fights broke out during matches.

Disgusted by the behavior of players who were supposed to be "gentlemen," the officers of the New England Association of National Base Ball Players elected to simply withdraw the prize, melt it down, and sell the metal. In 1868, the ball was taken to a silversmith who carried out the Association's wishes. The Silver Ball was melted down

By the time of this 1869 game on the Green of Washington, Connecticut, the "New England" style of baseball had nearly vanished. The modern layout of the playing field is easily recognizable. During the game pictured, alumni of The Gunnery School defeated a team from nearby Woodbury, 71–15. *Photo courtesy of the Connecticut Historical Society, Hartford, Connecticut.*

and sold for $19.46, which went into the Association's treasury. The results of seventeen championship match games were engraved on the trophy at the time it was destroyed.

Baseball was changing as the 1860s drew to a close, and the struggle to maintain the amateur status of the game was a losing one. Particularly skillful players were recruited from other teams and secretly paid for their services. Fewer games were played on public grounds like Boston Common, and more were played in enclosed parks where admission could be charged. And many of those who came to watch the games were less interested in seeing "good form" than in having the team they had wagered on come out victorious and win them a few dollars.

The melting of the Silver Ball was but one sign that baseball was no longer a gentlemanly pursuit. The game was about to become a business.

(2)

1870–1879:
Playing for Pay

The Cincinnati Red Stockings shocked the baseball world in 1869 by openly fielding a team made up entirely of professional ballplayers (who received salaries of $600 to $1,400 for the season). Many baseball players had received money prior to this, either as inducement to jump to a new club or for their work on the field, but the practice was frowned upon and such payments were not publicized. The Red Stockings toured the country from coast-to-coast, winning 56 games without a loss in 1869, and extending their winning streak through the first 27 games of 1870. Among the cities they visited were Boston, Lowell, Pittsfield, Springfield, and Worcester.

The unprecedented success of the Cincinnati club provided a tremendous boost to the game. New fans were introduced to baseball as the remarkable winning streak received national attention. Businessmen and boosters in other cities began to raise money for professional teams of their own. And players were finally able to consider baseball as a legitimate profession.

In March of 1871, representatives of ten clubs met to form the first professional league: the National Association of Professional Base Ball Players. The Association lasted five years, until the National League was launched in 1876. In the late 1870s, other professional leagues, now ranked as minor leagues, were organized.

Rules of the 1870s differed drastically from those of today. Pitchers threw from a box located only 45 feet from the batter; they could take a running start before releasing the ball, but their motion was restricted to an underhand delivery. Batters could call for a high pitch (waist to shoulder) or a low pitch (knee to waist). It took nine called balls to draw a walk, and sometimes many more pitches than that, for umpires were not required to make any call on pitches they weren't sure about. A foul ball caught on the first bounce was an out, but batters could reach base on a "fair-foul" hit: a ball was fair and in play as long as it first struck the ground in fair territory even if it subsequently went foul. Some players became proficient at the fair-foul hit much as later players mastered the bunt. Modifications to the rules were made during this decade: in 1873 players were prohibited from catching balls in their caps, the batter's box was introduced in 1874, and the fair-foul hit was eliminated in 1877.

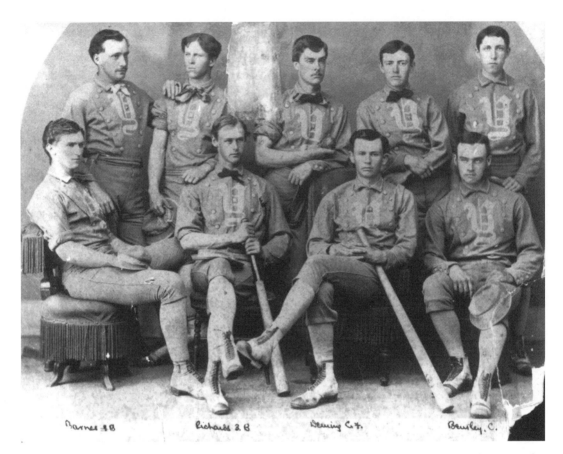

The Yale University Base Ball Club was organized in 1865, and played its first match against the Agallian Club of Wesleyan University in September of that year, defeating the Agallians 39-13. In 1868, the first annual Harvard–Yale game was played. The 1871 Yale team pictured here suffered the school's fourth straight loss to Harvard. Yale students attributed the loss to poor scheduling and final exams: "By the same mismanagement as in the previous year, Yale ventured to risk a Harvard game when her players were demoralized by annual examinations." In its ninth attempt, on July 14, 1874, Yale finally defeated its rival from Cambridge, 4–0—the first time Harvard had ever been shut out by a college team. *Photo courtesy of the Yale University Library Manuscripts and Archives.*

Amateur baseball clubs struggled to survive in the 1870s. It became a matter of civic pride that a city could afford to acquire and support a professional nine; home-grown teams that played simply for the love of the game were relegated to a lesser status. In an attempt to sustain the amateur game, the National Association of Amateur Base Ball Players was formed in 1871; it quickly fell apart when its member clubs couldn't agree on whether or not to charge admission to their games. Teams that had been powerhouses in the 1860s started to break up. The Boston Lowells, once the most heralded club in New England, disbanded at the end of the 1873 season, and other amateur nines soon followed.

Sept. 28, 1870: The Name Game

The earliest record of an organized African-American baseball club in New England is an account of a Boston game between two teams, both named the Resolutes. One was an all-black team, and the other all-white. The two clubs agreed to a match, with the terms that the losing team would have to relinquish the Resolutes name. The *Boston Herald* reported the outcome:

> *A game for the possession of the name was played between the two Resolute clubs (white and colored) of this city, on the Union Grounds yesterday afternoon. The colored boys went first to the bat, but made only one run, which was doubled by the whites in their first inning. At the close of the fifth inning the score stood 13 to 8 in favor of the white nine, but as the game progressed they lost this advantage, and were finally defeated, 25 to 15. They found the pitching of their opponents very hard to hit, and in the field they showed playing which deserved to deprive them of their name. They succeeded in making one very good double play during the game, but the greater part of their fielding was inferior to that of the descendants of Ham.*
>
> *Following is the score of the game:*

COLORED	O.	R.		WHITE	O.	R.
Gregory, p.	3	4		Clark, r. f.	0	4
Banfield, s. s.	3	4		McCann, 2 b.	1	1
Churchill, 2 b.	3	3		Cuddy, c.	5	0
Cruckendle, c. f.	3	3		Prime, c. f.	4	1
Shepard, l. f.	3	3		Mason, 1 b	4	1
Humphrey, 1 b	2	2		Foley, l. f.	5	1
W. Taylor, c	4	1		Dever, s. s.	2	3
Molineaux, 3 b	2	3		Malone, 3 b.	3	2
J. Taylor, r. f.	4	2		McLaughlin, p.	3	2
Total	27	25		Total	27	15

INNINGS

	1	2	3	4	5	6	7	8	9		
Colored	1	6	1	0	0	5	3	7	2	—	25
White	2	2	5	3	1	1	0	1	0	—	15

Umpire—Mr. Tompkins of the King Philip Club. Time—2 hours, 35 minutes.

There is no record of what name the losing team chose to adopt. The victors continued to play in the Boston area. In May 1871, the Resolutes faced another all-black team, the Auroras of Chelsea, in what one of the sporting papers described as "an excellent game."

Above: The 1873 Amherst College baseball team. Fourteen years after Amherst won baseball's first intercollegiate contest, this squad demonstrates that the school's players are no longer in a state of "undress." *Photo courtesy of the Amherst College Archives. Below:* 1874 game action at Wesleyan University in Middletown, Connecticut. The pitcher is in his windup, about to deliver the ball underhand to the batter (in light trousers). The rules of the time required that the pitcher's hand pass below his hip on the forward motion. *Photo courtesy of Transcendental Graphics.*

College baseball clubs were the most prominent ones still upholding the amateur tradition, but even on campus professionalism wasn't entirely excluded. Since neither college nines nor league teams were constrained by fixed schedules, there were many exhibition games between students and professionals, and an increasing overlap developed between the two groups. The better college players occasionally moonlighted for professional teams, and professional players were sometimes brought in as ringers on the college teams.

An attempt to establish eligibility guidelines for college players was made in 1879 when the Intercollegiate Baseball Association was formed. Member clubs were Amherst, Brown, Dartmouth, Harvard, Princeton and Yale. Yale, however, withdrew from the Association when the other clubs voted to prohibit the use of players who had been on professional nines.

By the late 1870s, newspaper coverage of baseball included information on gate receipts, player salaries, owner profits, and contract disputes. Baseball was firmly established as a business venture.

BOSTON RED STOCKINGS

The birth of baseball's first major league in 1871 also marked the debut of the only professional ball club to continue uninterrupted to the present day. A charter franchise of the National Association, the Boston Red Stockings switched to the National League in 1876 as the "Red Caps." The team went through name changes including "Beaneaters," "Doves," and "Rustlers" before becoming the Boston "Braves" in 1913. After a move to Milwaukee in 1953, the club went on to Atlanta in 1966 where it operates today.

Toward the end of the 1870 season, the newly formed Boston Base Ball Association determined to field a professional nine that would be the finest in the country. To that end, club president Ivers Adams induced Cincinnati Red Stockings manager Harry Wright to come to Boston and put together a team. For his services, Wright was offered a salary of $2,500, more than double what he had been paid by Cincinnati. Despite the Red Stockings' phenomenal performance on the field, the team had failed to show a sufficient profit; as a result, the Cincinnati directors elected to discontinue paying their players and revert to amateur status. This left Harry Wright free to accept the Boston deal.

Wright was given full authority to assemble and manage the new Boston team. His first act was to bring with him from Cincinnati his brother George, the team's shortstop (and highest paid player), as well as right fielder Cal McVey and first baseman Charlie Gould, who had been the Red Stockings' only native Cincinnatian. Wright also appropriated the "Red Stockings" name for his new team. Three more imports from the Midwest were added to the club: pitcher Al Spalding, outfielder Fred Cone, and second baseman Ross Barnes, all of whom had been playing for the Forest City Club of Rockford, Illinois.

Harry Wright was not simply concerned with forming a team, but with organizing a professional league. At the founding meeting of the National Association on March 17, 1871, Wright was selected to head the league's steering committee. He turned out to be the guiding figure throughout the Association's five-year history. Wright's determination to make the first professional league a success was so consuming that his contemporaries often referred to the National Association as "Harry Wright's League." Later, historians from Henry Chadwick to Harold Seymour anointed Wright with the title "father of professional baseball."

Wright's character was something of a throwback to the gentlemanly era of baseball: he was a soft-spoken, modest man who avoided profanity, tobacco, and liquor. He bore a number of responsibilities, both for the Association and for his team. Wright served as the Red Stockings' captain, manager, center fielder, and relief pitcher. At that time, the captain was the man charged with game strategy; the manager acted primarily as a business manager, scheduling games, making travel plans, finding accommodations, and negotiating salaries.

Given a free hand and $15,000 for payroll and expenses, Harry Wright assembled some of the finest talent in baseball for the 1871 Boston Red Stockings.

Wright's younger brother George had been the star of the Cincinnati team. He was a strong hitter, a daring base runner, and fielded his shortstop position so gracefully that he made it seem effortless. George was more outgoing than Harry and less modest. Handsome, single, and dashing, George Wright was treated like a stage star; he was showered with gifts, worshipped by youngsters, and was a favorite of the press and the ladies.

Tall right-handed pitcher Albert Spalding also became a favorite, soon eclipsing George Wright in popularity among Boston fans. Although he never learned to throw a curve ball, Spalding possessed a blazing fastball and pinpoint control. He went on to lead the league in wins during every season of the National Association's existence, totaling 205 victories and only 53 losses in five years. Spalding had been something of a baseball prodigy: at age 16, while with the Rockford Forest Citys, he had already been proclaimed "the best pitcher in the West." After joining the Boston team, the twenty-year-old Spalding quickly proved himself to be the best pitcher anywhere.

Several other members of the 1871 club were also standouts at their positions. Flamboyant Ross Barnes was rated by Henry Chadwick as "the model second baseman." Like George Wright, Barnes was a complete player—brilliant in the field, on the basepaths, and at the plate, where he was the acknowledged master of the "fair-foul" hit. Young catcher Cal McVey, who kept in shape by boxing, was a versatile player who could field any position and was always among the league leaders in batting. Charlie Gould, a former bookkeeper in his father's butter and egg business, was one of the weaker hitters on the club but a stellar first baseman (a difficult position to play in the days before gloves).

Two weeks after the March organizational meeting of the National Association, the Red Stockings were in Boston, working out several hours a day at the Tremont Gymnasium. After a series of exhibition games in April, the team played its first official game on May 5, beating the Washington Olympics 20-18 at Washington's Olympics Grounds. A *Boston Herald* report on the season opener included mention of the gambling that had become commonplace: "The game of this afternoon has been the theme of discussion, speculation and excitement in base ball circles ever since the opening of the season, and it is understood in sporting circles that a heavy pile of lucre changed hands because of the results." Boston's first home game was played before 3,000 spectators on May 16; with George Wright out of the line-up, the Red Stockings suffered a 20-14 defeat at the hands of the Troy Haymakers.

Boston's home field was the South End Grounds, also known as the Walpole Street Grounds and the Union Grounds. The park was of rough, wooden construction with a capacity of about 6,000. Most National Association ballparks permitted the sale of liquor as well as betting pools similar to those used in horse racing (Brooklyn's Union Grounds even had a special luxury section reserved for gamblers). While other teams were plagued by fights among spectators and the influence of bookmakers, Boston largely avoided these problems by prohibiting both liquor and betting at the South End Grounds.

Although heavily favored to win the championship, the Red Stockings got off to a slow start, struggling to play .500 ball through the first half of the season. The team was beset with injuries, including serious ones to George Wright and Cal McVey. Like most clubs of the era, the Red Stockings had only one substitute on its roster. In July, when too many of his players were injured to field a team, Harry Wright had to cancel more than two weeks of scheduled games in order to give them time to heal. One of

This 1875 photograph taken inside Boston's South End Grounds provides a superb view of the park's crude construction. The teams are the visiting Philadelphia Athletics (left) and the Red Stockings, who would win a fourth straight National Association championship. The Boston players are: (standing, from right) Harry Wright, Cal McVey, George Wright, Al Spalding, Deacon White, and (seated, from right) Harry Schafer, Ross Barnes, Jim O'Rourke, Andy Leonard. *Photo courtesy of the Boston Public Library, Print Department*

the few players to avoid injury was third baseman Harry Schafer, who manned the hot corner for Boston in each of its five seasons, playing every one of the team's games until midway through 1875.

In August and September, Boston made a strong drive for the pennant, finishing the season with a record of 20 wins, 10 losses, and 1 tie. The Philadelphia Athletics and Chicago White Stockings chalked up similar records, however, and a champion wasn't determined until mid-November. Because of the lack of a fixed league schedule, the Championship Committee was unsure which games should be counted in the final standings. Teams played a different number of games, some victories were actually forfeits gained from teams that had folded during the season, and other games were merely exhibition matches. It wasn't even certain whether the championship should be determined on the basis of most wins or highest winning percentage. The pennant was finally awarded to Philadelphia, much to the disappointment of Red Stockings and White Stockings fans (Chicago was the sentimental favorite for the pennant because they had lost their park, uniforms, and equipment during the great fire and had to play the balance of the year on the road).

Individually, Boston players dominated the league. Al Spalding led the Association in wins; Cal McVey, George Wright, and Ross Barnes all batted over .400; McVey led the league in hits and Barnes led in runs scored.

Harry Wright was determined to win the 1872 championship, and bolstered his outfield by the addition of another Cincinnati veteran, Andy Leonard. Leonard, a former hatter who had played for Washington in 1871, was a sure-handed fielder and possessed one of baseball's strongest throwing arms.

The Red Stockings got off to a 18 and 1 start, including 15 wins in a row, and easily took the 1872 pennant with a final record of 39 and 8. It was to be the first of four straight championships.

Harry Wright still wasn't satisfied and continued to improve his team. For the 1873 roster, he picked up two young men who were to be among the outstanding ballplayers of the 19th century: Orator Jim O'Rourke and Deacon White. O'Rourke, who had begun his professional career with the short-lived Middletown Mansfields the year before, replaced Charlie Gould at first base. Deacon White, a man of temperate character, took over the catching chores, forming with Al Spalding the most accomplished battery in baseball. A month into the season, Wright also acquired veteran Bob "The Magnet" Addy for the outfield.

Wright didn't stop at acquiring ballplayers. Once he had them, he worked them hard, exercising them in the gymnasium and on the playing field. Pre-game batting and fielding practice were among Harry Wright's training innovations. He also worked himself hard; in addition to his business responsibilities, Wright continually strove to improve his team's playing skills and develop new game strategies. Wright himself was the Association's leading relief pitcher, revolutionizing that role by using it as a strategy instead of a last resort. He found that after opposing batters had faced Al Spalding's blazing fastballs for most of the game, they could be thrown off-stride by Wright's "dew drop" change-ups in the late innings.

After the 1874 season, Harry Wright rarely played, and relinquished the role of field captain to Al Spalding. Wright instead concentrated on his managerial duties and the team's business affairs.

Boston won the 1873, 1874, and 1875 championships by increasing margins over their competition, posting a record of 71 and 8 in their final year—a season in which they were undefeated at home with a 37-0 record in the South End Grounds. The Red Stockings of 1873 to 1875 included four future Hall-of-Famers: Harry Wright, George Wright, Jim O'Rourke, and Al Spalding (Deacon White probably should be a fifth member of the Hall). They dominated the league so completely that public interest in the pennant races waned. Although the league was plagued by other problems as well (gambling, poor umpiring, erratic schedules), to some extent the Red Stockings fell victim to their own success, and the National Association collapsed after the 1875 season.

MIDDLETOWN MANSFIELDS

Connecticut's first major league baseball team was admitted to the National Association in 1872 for only one reason: the club sent in the required ten-dollar entrance fee.

The Middletown Mansfields, named for Civil War General Joseph Mansfield, had been organized as a junior amateur team in 1866. Although the Mansfields billed themselves as the champions of Connecticut, they were far below the caliber of the professional clubs, and there was strong resistance to their entry into the Association. The Mansfields were admitted when league officials realized that there was no provision for rejecting clubs as long as the clubs paid the ten-dollar fee.

As the Mansfields made the transition from amateur to professional, the team's management made an effort to strengthen its roster. One of the acquisitions was first baseman Tim Murnane of Naugatuck, Connecticut. Murnane would lead the 1872 Middletown team in batting with a .339 average, and then go on to play for Boston and Providence in the National League. Later, he would serve as president of the minor New England League and become sports editor of the *Boston Globe*. Another helpful addition was John Clapp, a strong-armed catcher who was one of the first backstops to play close behind the batter. Clapp would later play 212 consecutive games in the National League; for a catcher, in the days before protective equipment, that was considered an iron man achievement.

The most important find was Jim O'Rourke, a young amateur shortstop from Bridgeport. O'Rourke went on to have one of the most remarkable careers in baseball history—his professional playing career alone spanned *forty* years—and he was later enshrined in the Baseball Hall of Fame. Debuting with the Mansfields in 1872, O'Rourke made his last major league appearance in 1904, catching a complete game at age 54. In 1912, aged *62*, he caught a game for New Haven in the Connecticut League. Called "Orator Jim" because of his reputation as a clubhouse lawyer, O'Rourke did earn a law degree from Yale in 1887, while still a full-time ballplayer. In addition to a spectacular playing career, Jim O'Rourke served one year as a National League umpire and five years as president of the Connecticut League.

Although Middletown performed stronger than expected on the field, they were simply outclassed by the other teams and underfinanced. Not even the late addition of veteran pitcher Asa "Count" Brainard, ace of the old Cincinnati Red Stockings, could help. With a team record of 5 wins and 19 losses, the Mansfields folded in August, lasting less than one season as a professional franchise.

The Mansfield Club Grounds, where Middletown played its home games, later became the site of the Connecticut Hospital for the Insane.

HARTFORD DARK BLUES

Connecticut re-entered the major leagues in 1874, when the Hartford Dark Blues joined the National Association.

With most of the better professional players already on the rosters of established teams, the Dark Blues had difficulty putting together a line-up. They finally assembled a large enough collection of journeymen and has-beens to field a team. Lip Pike, a power hitter and adept fielder, was signed to captain the club and play center field. Second baseman Bob Addy was picked up from the Boston Red Stockings, Jim Tipper of the defunct Mansfields joined Pike in the outfield, Ev Mills manned first base, and Civil War veteran Scott Hastings did duty as the team's catcher.

Hartford sought in vain for a competent pitcher; instead, they had to settle for the peripatetic Cherokee Fisher. Fisher had pitched for three different teams in the National Association's first three seasons, with a cumulative record of 17 wins and 21 losses. He was gifted with a blazing fastball but wasn't always sober enough to get it over the plate.

The new ball club also had difficulty securing a home field. Not until March, with the season due to begin the following month, did the Dark Blues settle on a Willys Avenue site near Colt's Rifle Works. As it turned out, inhospitable New England weather gave Hartford extra time anyway: as late as April 26, six inches of snow covered the playing field. After heroic efforts to get the diamond in suitable shape, the first game at the Hartford Ball Club Grounds finally took place on May 1.

After a surprisingly strong early run, the Dark Blues skidded lower and lower in the standings for the rest of the season. One of the few bright spots was the batting of Lip Pike, who hit .340 and led the league in doubles and slugging average. Hartford's numerous low points in 1874 included a game in which the team committed *28* errors. Even more embarrassing was the club's pitching: Cherokee Fisher was twice suspended for drunkenness and replaced by Bill Stearns, who won 2 games and lost 14 (Stearns was one of the least successful pitchers in baseball history; his lifetime batting average of .191 in five seasons is actually higher than his career winning percentage of .158 in 76 decisions). Fisher ended his first and last season with Hartford with a record of 14 and 23. The team as a whole finished the year in seventh place, 27 1/2 games behind the pennant-winning Red Stockings

Hartford's fortunes changed dramatically in 1875, when local banker and aspiring politician Morgan G. Bulkeley became the club's chief financial backer.

Lip Pike departed and veteran Bob "Death to Flying Things" Ferguson was brought in as manager, captain, and third baseman (while already serving as the National

The 1875 Hartford Dark Blues, during the National Association's final season. The next year, the club became a charter franchise of the new National League. Seated in the center of the photograph is manager and third baseman Bob Ferguson. Long before ballplayers had candy bars named after them, cigars called "Captain Bobs" were being sold in Hartford to capitalize on the popularity of the Dark Blues manager. The tyrannical but multi-talented Ferguson was also the Association's president (the only active player ever to serve in such a role) and often umpired games. *Photo courtesy of Transcendental Graphics.*

Association's president). Ferguson was a respected baseball man who had captained the Brooklyn Atlantics nine that put an end to the Cincinnati Red Stockings' winning streak in 1870. He ran his teams with an iron hand and had no tolerance for the shoddy play and poor habits that had afflicted the Dark Blues in 1874.

Ev Mills continued to play first base. Shoring up the rest of the infield were "Black Jack" Burdock, a slick-fielding second baseman, and shortstop Tom Carey, who had been captain of the New York Mutuals.

A completely new outfield was put in place, consisting of Tom York, Jack Remsen, and rookie "Yaller Bill" Harbidge.

Replacing Cherokee Fisher on the mound was a two-man rotation—unusual for those days, when a pitcher was expected to work every game the same as any other player. The team's number one pitcher was Candy Cummings, a little 120-pound right-hander who was the foremost practitioner of the curveball (his claim to have invented the pitch later got him voted into the Hall of Fame). The second pitcher was Tommy Bond, a 19-year-old native of Ireland with a delivery so fast that he often injured his catchers.

The Dark Blues quickly demonstrated that they were not the same team that had represented Hartford the year before. The club won its first twelve games of the season, putting them in a solid second place, behind 16–0 Boston. Ferguson's team didn't lose until May 18, when the Red Stockings bested them by a score of 10–5.

During the first couple of months of the season, Candy Cummings did most of the pitching while Tommy Bond played right field. During practices, however, Cummings taught Bond the curveball, and by mid-season the younger pitcher was taking a regular turn on the mound.

Although not a single member of the team batted .300, good defense and superb pitching by Cummings and Bond secured a strong third-place finish for the Dark Blues, with a final record of 54 wins and 28 losses. Candy Cummings was 35–12 and Tommy Bond's mark was 19–18; together, the two Hartford pitchers combined to lead the league with 13 shutouts.

The National Association received its death blow in February 1876. William Hulbert, president of the Chicago White Stockings, proposed a new organization to be known as The National League of Professional Base Ball Clubs. No longer an association of *players*, the new league would be controlled by the investors who operated the clubs.

Hulbert's goal was to put professional baseball on a sound business footing and bring respectability to the game. With the support of Boston's Harry Wright and Hartford owner Morgan Bulkeley, the National League moved quickly to correct the problems that had beleaguered the old Association. Prospective franchises had to be located in cities with populations of at least 75,000 (an exception was made for Hartford), the entry fee for new teams was raised to $100, and no club could be located within five miles of another league team. The league also took steps to improve the game's image: gambling, pool-selling, and liquor sales were forbidden in all parks; admission prices were set at a steep fifty cents to attract a more prosperous clientele; a professional umpiring staff was established with umpires earning a generous $5 per game.

Although Hulbert was the driving force behind the league, he felt it was important to have an easterner as head of the organization. Names of candidates were put in a hat, and Hartford's Morgan Bulkeley was chosen by lot to be the first president of the National League.

Having jettisoned the financially shaky clubs, the inaugural season opened with an eight-team league (there had been thirteen teams during the last year of the National Association).

Hartford fielded essentially the same line-up as in 1875. One of the few differences was that Tommy Bond had become the Dark Blues' ace pitcher, winning 31 games, while Candy Cummings posted 16 wins as the number two man on the staff. The club finished the 1876 season in the same place as they had the year before: third. But they beat out the Boston Red Stockings, who ended up in fourth place, nine games behind Hartford.

The year was not a financial success for the Dark Blues, partly because they were located in the league's smallest city. For the 1877 season, Hartford arranged to play its home games in Brooklyn's fabled Union Grounds, which had opened in 1862 as baseball's first enclosed ballpark.

May 18, 1875: The Great Base Ball Match

After a 1874 season that ended with the Hartford Dark Blues in seventh place, the Connecticut team did a complete reversal in the spring of 1875. Hartford won its first dozen games, and hopes rose that the Dark Blues could prevent Boston from winning a fourth consecutive title. On May 18, the two teams faced each other on Hartford's Ball Club Grounds. Both teams were putting perfect records on the line—Hartford at 12–0, and the Red Stockings with a 16–0 mark. In its morning edition, the *Hartford Courant* predicted a large turnout:

THE GREAT GAME TODAY

The culminating point of the season will be reached to-day in the meeting of the Bostons and Hartfords in this city. The game will probably attract the largest crowd that ever attended a base ball match in Hartford. All the reserved seats in the pavilion have been sold for to-day, and the stand on the east side will be reserved for those wishing seats there.

The next day, the *Courant* reported the disappointing results. Although the outcome wasn't a happy one for Hartford fans, more than 9,000 spectators turned out to support their team:

The Hartfords Sustain Their First Defeat, the Bostons Being the Victors by a Score of 10 to 5—A Hotly Contested Game, and One Rather Unsatisfactory to Hartford People

On Tuesday the much talked of and long looked for contest between the Hartfords and Bostons took place on the grounds in Hartford, in the presence of the largest audience ever assembled in New England to witness a contest for superiority between two rival base ball nines. Large delegations were present from Boston, New York, Providence, New Haven, Middletown, New Britain, Waterbury, Springfield, and all the smaller towns in this vicinity. The city appeared as it does on holiday, and by three o'clock the streets were nearly deserted, everybody who was so fortunate as to secure a seat, and many who were not, having gone to the ball grounds. The works of the Case, Lockwood & Brainerd company, Colts, Pratt & Whitney, Kellogg & Bulkeley Lithograph company, and other firms being closed to allow their employees to witness the match, which has been the all-absorbing topic of conversation for weeks.

The fans and the *Courant* both attributed the loss in part to the umpire. The newspaper was a bit more circumspect in its criticism, however:

Mr. Alphonse Martin, of the Nameless club of New York, was the gentleman decided upon as umpire, and though some of his decisions were against the home club, there was no excuse for the hissing, hooting, and continued insult that was heaped upon him, for he undoubtedly decided the points according to the best of his ability, though he was materially helped in one or two instances in his decisions by Spaulding, who captains the Boston team, since Harry Wright retired. But this must always be expected, as the Bostons are noted in this respect, all umpires apparently holding the champions in awe, and fearing to decide against them in a close or disputed point.

The newspaper report concluded by advocating a peculiar batting strategy and by blasting Hartford first baseman Ev Mills:

The Hartfords, too, lacked the nerve and coolness which have heretofore characterized their play, evidently being a trifle afraid of their opponents, and very deficient in base running. Another thing noticeable in contrast with the Bostons' play is that they are not as careful as they should be in batting. They are apt to hit a ball at the wrong time. Better far to have a strike called, or as the Bostons do, strike at a ball with the intention of frightening the catcher, rather than hitting it, than to force a base runner out at second or third bases. Mills, who is weakest in this respect, lost the game, giving the Bostons their three runs in the first inning, by his stupidity, rather than carelessness, but he brought in two of the five runs in the fourth inning by his safe batting. He is the weak spot in the nine, and should try and improve his play, and obtain some of the enthusiasm which prevails to a very great extent with all the other players.

The following detailed score will give full particulars of the game:—

HARTFORD	O.	R.	1B.	T.B.	P.O.	A.	E.	BOSTONS	O.	R.	1B.	T.B.	P.O.	A.	E.
Allison, c	3	1	1	1	2	1	0	G. Wright, s s	2	2	4	5	1	0	0
Burdock, 2b	4	1	1	1	1	7	3	Barnes, 2b	3	2	2	2	4	4	0
Carey, s s	5	0	1	1	0	2	0	O'Rourke, 3b	2	3	2	2	2	5	1
Cummings, p	3	0	1	1	0	1	0	Leonard, l f	5	0	0	0	4	0	0
York, l f	3	1	2	2	3	0	0	McVey, c f	3	1	1	1	2	0	0
Ferguson, 3b	3	1	1	1	2	3	0	Spaulding, p	3	0	2	2	1	5	0
Remsen, c f	1	1	1	1	3	0	1	White, c	3	0	0	0	3	1	1
Mills, 1b	2	0	1	1	14	0	2	Manning, r f	3	1	1	1	0	0	1
Bond, r f	3	0	0	0	2	0	0	Latham, 1b	3	1	1	1	10	0	1
Totals	27	5	9	9	27	14	6	Totals	27	10	13	14	27	15	4

INNINGS

Hartfords	0	0	0	5	0	0	0	0	0	—	5
Bostons	3	0	2	0	0	0	2	0	3	—	10

Earned runs, Bostons, 3; bases on errors, Hartfords, 3, Bostons, 1; left on bases, Hartfords, 3, Bostons, 4; time of game, 2 hours and 12 minutes; balls called on Cummings, 7, on Spaulding, 5; umpire, Alphonse Martin of the Nameless club of New York.

Among those present at the match was Hartford resident Mark Twain, who suffered the misfortune of having his umbrella stolen. Two days after the big game, the following announcement appeared in the *Courant*:

TWO HUNDRED AND FIVE DOLLARS REWARD—At the great base ball match on Tuesday, while I was engaged in hurrahing, a small boy walked off with an English-made brown silk UMBRELLA belonging to me, and forgot to bring it back. I will pay $5 for the return of that umbrella in good condition to my house on Farmington avenue. I do not want the boy (in an active state) but will pay two hundred dollars for his remains. —SAMUEL L. CLEMENS.

Hartford finished the 1875 season in a respectable third place. Boston again won the championship, and their continued dominance of the National Association helped bring about the league's collapse that winter.

Despite the new location and yet another third-place finish in 1877, the club lost even more money and dropped out of the league at the end of the year.

Morgan Bulkeley served only one year as the league's nominal president. After the 1877 season, he left baseball to pursue his banking and political interests. He became president of Aetna Life Insurance Company, was elected mayor of Hartford, and later served as governor of Connecticut. However, by drawing the card that made him National League President during its inaugural season, Bulkeley was given baseball immortality with a plaque in the Hall of Fame.

NEW HAVEN ELM CITYS

The final season of the National Association had opened with a third entry from Connecticut: the New Haven Elm Citys, whose home field was the Howard Avenue Grounds.

Charlie Gould, veteran of the Cincinnati and Boston Red Stockings, served as captain and first baseman. Gould was one of the few capable players on a roster that was extremely shy of talent. The team included Sam Wright, younger brother of George and Harry, at shortstop; the similarity between Sam and George ended with their names—while George Wright batted .333 for Boston in 1875, Sam hit only .188 for New Haven. At center field for the Elm Citys was Jim Tipper, formerly with the Mansfields and Dark Blues (making him the only player to serve time with all three

Connecticut franchises); Tipper fared even worse than Sam Wright at the plate, hitting .158 on the season.

Despite some competent pitching by curveballer Tricky Nichols, the Elm Citys lost their first 15 games of the season, and 19 of their first 20. The high point of New Haven's solitary year as a major league franchise was an upset of the league-leading Boston team on July 2. The low points were numerous. In addition to the dreadful losing streak that began the season, New Haven at one point elected to forfeit a scheduled game with Hartford because the players were too disheartened from an 11–0 rout the day before.

Poor as their on-field performance was, even worse news came when two of the Elm City players—Billy Geer and Henry Luff—were arrested for burglarizing hotels in which the team stayed on road trips. Demonstrating how lax the National Association standards were, Geer was appointed to umpire a game two weeks later—while out on bail. Although the room shared by Geer and Luff was filled with stolen merchandise, both players were later acquitted of the charges and both continued their baseball careers.

Five teams disbanded during the National Association's final season, but New Haven stuck it out to the end (although the Elm Citys did fail to make a required tour of the league's western cities). New Haven wound up with a record of 7 wins and 40 losses, leaving them 48 games behind the 71–8 pennant-winning Boston Red Stockings.

BARB FENCE ARMOR.—The Boston Base Ball Grounds, enclosed with "Barb Armed" Fence.   (over)

This 1876 view of Boston's South End Grounds (in its first year as a National League ballpark) is from an advertising card distributed by the manufacturer of the barbed wire used atop the fence. The reverse side of the card includes a letter of endorsement from team president Nathan Apolonio, who states: "It saved us, on the afternoon of the first day it was put on, fifty dollars ($50) in special police and from $400 to $500 admission fees." Since admission was fifty cents and the park's capacity was about 6,000, Apolonio must have been expecting fifteen percent of the crowd to have entered by climbing the fence. *Photo courtesy of Elias Dudash.*

April 24, 1878: Bud Fowler Beats Boston

Twenty-year-old Bud Fowler began the 1878 season pitching for a semi-pro Chelsea, Massachusetts team. On April 24, the reigning National League champion Boston Red Caps faced a picked nine of local stars, including Fowler, in an exhibition game at South End Grounds. When Fowler stepped onto the field, he became the first African-American to play against a major league team in Boston. The pennant-winning Red Caps had not lost a single game so far, and were expecting an easy victory over the amateurs. Boston's star pitcher Tommy Bond had led league with 40 wins (and was on his way to another 40-win season). Some of the Boston players, including Bond and George Wright, didn't even bother to put on uniforms, playing in street clothes and ordinary shoes. Fowler held them to one run and the Red Caps suffered their first defeat of the year. The *Boston Post* provided a brief account of the game:

> *The Bostons played a game with a picked nine yesterday afternoon on the South End grounds and were beaten for the first time this season. Below is the score:—*

BOSTONS

	R.	1B.	P.O.	A.	E.
G. Wright, s.s.	1	0	0	1	1
Leonard, l. f.	0	0	0	0	0
O'Rourke, c. f.	0	1	1	0	0
Manning, r. f.	0	1	0	0	0
Sutton, 3b	0	0	0	0	0
Burdock, 2b	0	0	4	4	1
Morrill, 1b	0	1	12	0	1
Bond, p	0	0	0	8	1
Snyder, c	0	0	10	2	1
Totals	1	3	27	15	5

PICKED NINE

	R.	1B.	P.O.	A.	E.
Lynch, 2b	0	1	3	5	1
Flint, 3b	0	1	4	2	2
Foye, s. s.	0	0	1	7	0
Woods, r. f.	1	1	0	0	0
Gerrish, l. f.	1	1	1	0	1
Cook, 1b	0	0	15	0	0
Rollins, c.	0	0	3	2	3
Wilbur, c. f	0	0	0	0	0
Fowler, p	0	0	0	3	3
Totals	2	4	27	19	10

Innings	1	2	3	4	5	6	7	8	9		
Picked Nine	0	0	0	0	0	0	2	0	0	—	2
Bostons	1	0	0	0	0	0	0	0	0	—	1

> *Umpire—Mr. Schafer. First base on errors—Bostons 4, Picked Nine 2. Left on bases—Bostons 5, Picked Nine 4. Passed balls—Rollins 2. Bases on called balls—Bostons 1. Struck out—Manning, Snyder, Lynch (2), Flint, Gerrish (2). Two-base hit—Manning. Wild pitches—Fowler 2. Strikes called—Off Fowler 17, off Bond 13. Balls called—Off Fowler 15, off Bond 12. Strikes missed—Bostons 5, Picked Nine 15. Fowls [sic] struck—Bostons 9, Picked Nine 20. Time of game—1 hour 35 minutes.*

Three weeks after his victory over Boston, Bud Fowler became the first black to play in Organized Baseball. When the Lynn Live Oaks, of the minor league International Association, temporarily lost their regular pitcher to illness, they acquired Fowler from the Chelsea team. Fowler hurled three games for the Live Oaks, winning one. He ended the 1878 season with Worcester in National Association (no relation to the league that had folded in 1876). In 1879, Fowler pitched semi-pro ball for Malden in the Eastern Massachusetts League. Although described as "one of the best pitchers on the continent of America," Fowler was often released from clubs when other players refused to take the field with a black man. In a span of ten years, he played for seventeen teams in nine leagues. In 1887, Fowler was back in New England with Montpelier, Vermont in the North Eastern League. He was by then primarily a second baseman, and his status as team captain indicates that he was popular with both teammates and fans. Bud Fowler totaled 465 games in Organized Baseball, more than any African-American player of his century.

HARVARD MAGENTA

When the Harvard University Base Ball Club formed in 1864, the two players designated to select a uniform purchased gray French flannel for the shirts and brought the material to a Boston seamstress. They instructed her to embroider an old English "H" on the shirtfront in the school color, crimson. The students were surprised when they later picked up the outfits and found that she had instead used magenta for the school letter—the seamstress explained that magenta was "much more fashionable and much prettier" than crimson. The players (who were responsible for their own uniforms) couldn't afford to have them redone, so they took the field as the Harvard Magenta. The student body at the university was so delighted with the team's appearance, that the official school color was changed to magenta (until 1875, when crimson was re-adopted).

Wearing either color, the Harvard baseball team was not merely one of the best in New England, it was among the leading clubs in the country. Harvard was the only university nine to face the Cincinnati Red Stockings of 1869-70, playing them three times and faring as well as any of the other clubs that took on the professional team. In fact, Harvard nearly defeated the Red Stockings on their home turf. In the summer of 1870, the Magenta went on a tour of their own, taking on and defeating the Haymakers of Troy, N.Y., the Eckford Club of Syracuse, the Buffalo Niagaras, the Cleveland Forest Citys, and prominent clubs in Chicago, Milwaukee, Indianapolis, Washington, Baltimore, Philadelphia, and Brooklyn. During the course of the tour, on July 18, the Harvard club played the Red Stockings on Cincinnati's Union Grounds. The Magenta took a 17–12 lead into the ninth inning before losing 20–17.

One of the challenges that the Harvard ball club had to face came not from another team but from the head of their own school. In the early 1870s, university president

1877 Nine

	Dow		Lowell, *Mgr.*		Tower		Holmes
Ernst			Thayer, *Capt.*	Tyng		Wright	
Latham						Sawyer	

The 1877 Harvard team included Jim Tyng, who that year wore the first catcher's mask (on Tyng's knee in this photograph). The mask's inventor, team captain Fred Thayer, supposedly devised it in order to induce a reluctant Tyng to switch from outfield to catching. In those days of rough, barehanded baseball, Tyng took a great deal of ribbing for wearing a "cage" upon his face, but soon catchers everywhere were using the protective mask. Jim Tyng played seven seasons for Harvard's baseball team, his final one in 1879. That year, he graduated law school, passed the bar exam, and broke into the National League, pitching three games for Boston. *Photo courtesy of Transcendental Graphics.*

Charles W. Eliot threatened to close down the baseball program because he did not approve of the curve ball, calling it a "low form of cunning." As Eliot put it, "I heard that this year we won the championship because we have a pitcher who has a fine curve ball. I am further instructed that the purpose of the curve ball is to deliberately deceive the batter. Harvard is not in the business of teaching deception." Nor did Eliot care for pitchers who attempted to pick off base runners; he believed they were "ungentlemanly." In general, Eliot did approve of athletics, saying that they "supplied a new and effective force for resisting all sins which weaken or corrupt the body" and had the power to transform a "stooping, weak, and sickly youth into one well-formed, robust, and healthy." Eventually, the Harvard president was prevailed upon to let the baseball program continue, although his opinion of the game didn't improve with time. In early 1884, Eliot gave an address in which he said: "I think it a wretched game, but as an object of ambition for the youths to go to college, really it is a little weak. There are only nine men who can play the game, and there are 950 students in Harvard, and out of the nine there are but two desirable positions, I understand—pitcher and catcher—so there is little chance for the youth to gratify his ambition. I call it one of the worst games, although I know it is called the national game of the United States."

In the 1870s, the Harvard University nine continued to take on all comers, playing professional clubs from Hartford, Holyoke, New Bedford, New Haven, and Worcester—and twice defeating the champion Boston Red Stockings. The club's victories against the major league Boston team were among the highlights of the decade for the Cambridge students. Another was that the Magenta/Crimson defeated Yale every time that their archrivals ventured onto Harvard's Jarvis Field.

MINOR LEAGUES

The International Association, founded in 1877, is generally credited as baseball's first minor league although it never viewed itself as such. Leaders of the organization preferred to think of it as a rival to the National League. The Association was a fairly looseknit league with a wide geographic distribution (including New England, Ontario, Pittsburgh, and Columbus) that made travel and scheduling difficult.

At its inaugural meeting, Arthur "Candy" Cummings head of the Lynn, Massachusetts, Live Oaks was elected president. In six years as a pitcher in the old National Association and the National League, Cummings had won 145 games before returning to his home state to promote local baseball.

Teams drifted in and out of the Association. In the middle of the 1878 season, manager Frank Bancroft pulled his New Bedford team out of the league and embarked on a barnstorming tour. New Bedford played 130 games that year (at a time when National League teams played only 60 games in a season) and won the unofficial championship of New England.

In 1879, the league changed its name to the National Association because it no longer had any Canadian teams as members (which might have been a relief to the American teams since the Tecumsehs of London, Ontario had taken the league's first pennant). The following season was the league's last. During the International/National Association's four-year existence, New England was represented at various times by Hartford, Holyoke, Lowell, Lynn, Manchester, New Bedford, Springfield, and Worcester. Within a few years, there were dozens of active minor league teams in the region.

FROM RED STOCKINGS TO RED CAPS

If any team had good cause to oppose William Hulbert in his drive to form a new league it was the Boston Red Stockings. In the middle of the 1875 season, Hulbert violated National Association rules by signing Boston's "Big Four"—Al Spalding, Deacon White, Ross Barnes, and Cal McVey—to play for his own Chicago club the following year. The news devastated Boston fans, damaged team morale, and again illustrated the weakness of the Association which failed to enforce the prohibition against tampering.

Despite the illegal raid on his own team, however, Harry Wright recognized the inadequacies of the National Association and agreed with Hulbert's objectives in creating the National League. Wright threw his support behind the new enterprise and his considerable influence helped bring in other clubs.

The eight teams that comprised the National League in 1876 included six from the National Association and two new franchises. One of the new clubs was Cincinnati, which had finally re-entered the professional ranks. Perhaps as a courtesy to his old team, Harry Wright changed the Boston nickname from Red Stockings to Red Caps.

The inaugural season of the National League started well for Boston. Replacing Al Spalding on the mound was Joe Borden, a little right-hander who had hurled the major league's first no-hitter the year before. On April 22, 1876, Borden became the first pitcher to win a National League game, leading Boston to a 6–5 win over Philadelphia.

As the season progressed, the Red Caps slid down in the standings. Joe Borden's arm went sore; he posted a final record of 11 wins and 12 losses, and ended the season as Boston's groundskeeper (Harry Wright demanded that the injured Borden continue to earn his salary in some capacity). The team as a whole finished a poor fourth, 15 games behind pennant-winning Chicago.

Boston rebounded strongly the next year. Deacon White returned to the team and led the league in most batting categories. Ezra Sutton, a terrific third baseman with a rifle arm, played his first of twelve seasons with Boston. Pitcher Tommy Bond was picked up from Hartford and posted a league-leading total of 40 wins, his first of three consecutive 40-win seasons.

Behind Bond's pitching, the Red Caps won the National League championship in 1877 and repeated in 1878.

PROVIDENCE GRAYS

Rhode Island was a hotbed of baseball in the 1870s. Among the notable amateur clubs were the Bristols, the Cranston Atlantics, and the Providence Juniors, who played their home games at the Dexter Training Ground. Brown University consistently fielded teams that were among the country's finest college nines. Industrial teams were organized at the Rhode Island Locomotive Works and the Providence Tool Company, and local town teams throughout the state took part in exhibition games and tournaments.

In 1875, the semi-pro "Rhode Islands" were formed as an offshoot of the Providence Juniors. To properly house the new club, Rhode Island's first enclosed baseball grounds was constructed in Providence: Adelaide Park, near Broad Street on Adelaide Avenue.

Originally, the Rhode Islands' roster was made up almost entirely of local talent. Their first year was such a success, however, that the club's investors offered contracts to the best players they could get from anywhere in the country. The 1876 team included third baseman Tom Burns, who later played thirteen years in the National League, and future Hall-of-Famer Ned Hanlon.

The Rhode Islands improved further in 1877, after fiery little manager Dickey Pearce completely revamped the roster. The opening day pitcher was Hugh "One Arm" Daily, who six years later pitched a no-hitter in the National League and the year after that tied a record by striking out 19 batters in a game. Another pitcher for the Rhode Islands was local favorite Fred Cory from South Kingston; Corey went on to

May 8, 1878: A Brilliant Triple Play

In the week since Messer Park opened as home of Providence's new National League franchise, the Grays had split two games with Boston. When the teams met for the third time (the third game in the Grays' history), interest was high and betting was heavy. As reported in the *Providence Journal* the following day:

> As was anticipated, the third contest for the League Championship Pennant, between the Bostons and Providence nine, at the Messer Street Park yesterday afternoon, attracted between four and five thousand spectators. Herrick & Tonge's Band enlivened the occasion with choice selections of music, and a strong detail of police officers under Captain McKenzie, preserved the utmost good order in and around the park. Previous to the game, pools were selling down town in the ratio of 2 to 1 in favor of the Bostons, and the result of the game doubtless surprised many of the visiting money-catchers, who departed leaving a large portion of the shekels in the hands of the backers of the Providence nine.

But fans were treated to more than a Providence win. They became witnesses to a play that has been the subject of debate for over a century: a triple play initiated by Grays center fielder Paul Hines. In the bottom of the eighth inning (the home team didn't always bat last in those days), Boston had two runners on base—Jack Manning on third and Ezra Sutton on second—with no outs. As the *Journal* described the play:

> Burdock struck the ball, lifting it over Carey's head, sufficiently far to warrant the base-runners, and even the anxious crowd in prophesying that it was a base hit. Manning and Sutton speeded to the home plate, while fear and trembling possessed the hearts of the breathless spectators. But Hines, meantime, had espied the ball, and running at the top of his speed from far centrefield, captured it ere it touched the ground, ceased not his running until he had touched third, thus, unassisted, putting out both Burdock and Manning, and then threw swiftly to Sweasey, retiring Sutton, and COMPLETING A BRILLIANT TRIPLE PLAY, amid the wildest shouts and demonstrations of delight imaginable. The runners looked at each other in blank astonishment at this wonderful play, while the crowd, knowing that Hines had saved the day, cheered and shouted without stint or restraint. The members of the nine expressed their delight at the play by sundry slaps and demonstrations of pleasure, all of which "Paul" received with becoming modesty. It was a long time ere the crowd became sufficiently composed to resume their attention upon the game.

The paper's box score credited Hines with two putouts and an assist on the play:

PROVIDENCE	A.B.	R.	1B.	T.B.	L.	P.O.	A.	E.
Higham, rf	4	1	1	1	0	2	1	0
York, lf	4	1	1	1	1	1	0	0
Murnan, 1b	4	0	0	0	0	9	0	2
Hines, cf	4	0	1	1	2	4	1	0
Carey, ss	4	0	0	0	0	1	1	1
Hague, 3b	4	1	1	1	0	3	1	0
Nichols, p	4	0	0	0	0	0	7	2
Allison, c	4	0	3	4	3	6	1	2
Sweasey, 2b	4	0	0	0	0	1	2	1
Totals	36	3	7	8	6	27	6	8

BOSTONS	A.B.	R.	1B.	T.B.	L.	P.O.	A.	E.
Wright, ss	4	0	2	2	0	0	2	0
Leonard, lf	4	0	0	0	0	0	0	3
O'Rourke, cf	4	1	1	2	1	1	0	0
Manning, rf	3	0	0	0	0	1	0	1
Sutton, 3b	3	0	0	0	0	1	2	1
Burdock, 2b	4	1	0	0	0	4	4	0
Morrill, 1b	3	0	0	0	0	12	0	1
Bond, p	4	0	2	2	1	0	8	0
Snyder, c	4	0	0	0	0	8	1	6
Totals	33	2	5	6	2	27	15	12

INNINGS

	1	2	3	4	5	6	7	8	9		
Providence	1	0	0	0	0	0	1	1	0	—	3
Bostons	0	0	0	0	0	0	0	1	1	—	2

Umpire—J. A. Cross, Providence. Strikes called—off Nichols 18; Bond 10. Balls called—on Nichols 27; Bond 21; struck out—Murnan, Hague, Nichols (3), Sweasey, Manning, Sutton, Morrill, Bond; first base on errors—Providence 3, Bostons 4; passed balls—Allison 1; Snyder 5; triple play—Hines, Sweasey; double play—Burdock, Morrill; bases on called balls—Bostons 1; two-base hits—O'Rourke and Allison. Time of game—2 hours 55 minutes.

(Box score note: "L" stands for left on base.)

Hines later took credit for making the first *unassisted* triple play in baseball history, claiming that his throw to Charlie Sweasey at second hadn't been necessary. According to the rules of the time, if both runners had passed third base when Hines stepped on the bag, they were both immediately out and Hines had indeed turned an unassisted triple play. However, the other three men involved in the play—Sutton, Manning, and Sweasey—all later wrote the Sutton had been *on his way back to second* when Hines touched third base. The throw to Sweasey therefore had been necessary to make the third out, and the play was not unassisted. As Jim O'Rourke, who had scored earlier in that inning, later wrote, "The play itself was phenomenal, without the addition of other unreasonable 'phenoms'."

Oddly enough, Paul Hines was later credited with a distinction that he never claimed for himself: the Triple Crown (leading the league in batting average, home runs, and runs batted in) for his 1878 batting performance. At the time, RBIs were not yet considered a statistic and Abner Dalrymple was credited with the batting championship. As far as Hines knew, he'd only taken the home run championship—with four. Later research produced revised statistics and in 1968—*ninety years* after the fact—Hines was officially acknowledged as winning baseball's first Triple Crown.

play for three major league teams. The line-up also included veteran Charlie Sweasy at second base and Brown University star J. Lee Richmond in the outfield. Though long past his prime, 41-year-old Pearce manned shortstop himself.

The Rhode Islands performed well on the field and enjoyed a successful year. They drew large crowds as well as the attention of the National League. When the League elected to drop Hartford after the 1877 season, Providence was awarded a franchise to replace the Connecticut club.

In a break with tradition, the National League's newest addition adopted gray flannel instead of white for its home uniform, and the team became known as the "Grays." While the Providence Grays practiced at Dexter Training Ground in the spring of 1878, preparations were made to provide them with "the best baseball plant in the country." Construction on Messer Park began on April 1 and took exactly one month to complete; the final nail was hammered in a mere five minutes before the opening game got under way on May 1.

That opening day line-up included two players carried over from the semi-pro Rhode Islands: pitcher Fred Corey and second baseman Charlie Sweasy. New on the Providence roster were center fielder Paul Hines, who would be the only player to serve all eight seasons of the Grays' history, and first baseman Tim Murnane, who had played outfield for the pennant-winning Boston club the previous year. Joining the Grays from the defunct Hartford club were veterans Tom Carey at shortstop and Tom York in left field. In right field for Providence was Dick Higham, a heavy-hitting Englishman who had played for Hartford in 1876.

Through the first half of the 1878 season, Providence suffered from pitching problems. Fred Corey fell ill and was out for the year after winning only one game; Tricky Nichols "lost his skill entirely" according to the *Providence Journal,* posting a record of 4–7. The team then went through a succession of pitchers until 18-year-old John Montgomery Ward made his major league debut on July 15.

John Ward became one of the most influential figures in baseball history. A superb player, respected manager, and pioneering labor leader, Ward was eventually enshrined in the Baseball Hall of Fame.

In half a year with Providence, Ward garnered 22 wins against only 13 losses. The team finished in third place, with a 33–27 record.

There were a few major changes to the line-up the following year. Most important, George Wright and Jim O'Rourke came over to the Grays from the Red Caps. Their defection was one of the factors that later led Boston owner Arthur Soden to introduce the reserve clause that would bind players to their teams in perpetuity. Joining the team from Chicago, where he had led the National League in hits in 1878, was Joe "Old Reliable" Start, an exceptional fielding first baseman who had been playing organized baseball since 1860. Veteran curveball pitcher Bobby Matthews, who had won 131 games in five years with the National Association, was brought in as the club's second pitcher.

No longer with Providence were Charlie Sweasy, who retired after hitting only .175 the season before; Tom Carey, who became expendable when George Wright signed to play shortstop; and Dick Higham, who later became a National League

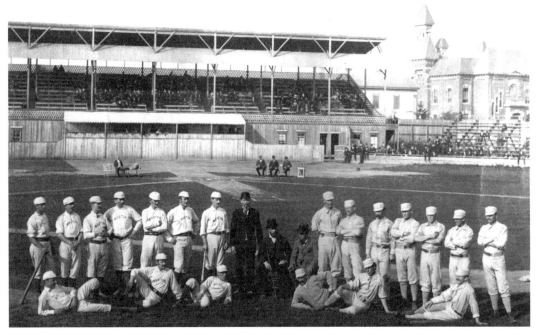

Providence's Messer Park in the spring of 1879. This marvelous view of the ballpark includes two pennant-winning teams: the 1878 National League champion Boston Red Stockings (left) and the Providence Grays (right) who went on to take the 1879 championship. At the time of its 1878 opening, Messer Park was one of the most modern ballparks in the country, with a seating capacity of 6,000, a wire screen behind home plate to protect spectators from foul balls, and an infield "as smooth as a billiard table." Note the lines of the pitcher's box in the center of the photo; at the time, pitchers delivered the ball from a four-by-six foot box located fifty feet from home plate. *Photo courtesy of the National Baseball Library & Archive, Cooperstown, N.Y.*

umpire—and earned the distinction of being the only major league umpire ever expelled for crookedness.

In addition to playing shortstop, George Wright served as the Grays manager in 1879, the only time in his career that he assumed the managerial reins. With his brother Harry still managing the Red Caps, an intense rivalry developed between the brothers, the teams, and the cities.

Through most of the season, a three-way battle for first place was fought between Providence, Boston, and Chicago. By September, the race was down to the teams managed by the Wright brothers, and at the end of the month George's team prevailed to take the pennant.

Due in large part to John Ward's pitching (his 47 wins and 239 strikeouts led the league in those categories), Providence finished the schedule five games ahead of Boston in the standings. The final game of the season was played on September 30 in Messer Park, where the Grays capped off the year by defeating the Red Caps 14-3.

The night after their final victory, a reception was held for the team at the Park Gardens on Broad Street. Hundreds of fans turned out to cheer their ball club. The Pawtucket Cornet Band provided music, a banquet was served in the pavilion, and "rivers of champagne" flowed all night. Mayor Doyle gave George Wright a floral bat and ball, and presented a gold medal to each member of the team. In only their second year as a major league franchise, the Providence Grays were the champions of baseball.

3

1880–1889:
Every City and Town, School and Factory

In the 1880s, baseball was at its zenith as the national pastime. The game was being played throughout the country by men, women, and children from every background, at every skill level. Amateur and semi-pro teams were fielded in towns and villages; cities scrambled to acquire professional franchises in the new leagues that were forming; the college game had spread to the women's schools; industrial leagues were formed at mills, shipyards, and factories.

The professional game continued to expand as businessmen and civic leaders started to see baseball as a viable commercial venture. A second major league, the American Association, started play in 1882; the Association, which had its greatest strength in midwestern cities, offered baseball at 25 cents admission (half the National League's price), and allowed liquor sales and Sunday games. In 1884, a third major league formed: the Union Association. Minor leagues increased in number from two in 1883 to seventeen only five years later. With so many leagues in competition, a "National Agreement" was formed between most of the associations; the agreement required member organizations to respect each other's contracts, specified the distinctions between "major" and "minor" leagues, and provided the basic structure for "Organized Baseball." As club owners set about establishing regulations for how ballplayers would be dealt with, the players began to organize themselves in an attempt to gain some protection from the edicts issued by management. In 1885, the Brotherhood of Professional Base Ball Players was formed, and the enduring conflict between owners and players escalated.

The 1880s were a busy decade for the rulesmakers. The number of called balls required for a base on balls was gradually reduced from eight in 1880 to four in 1889. In 1881, the pitching distance was increased from 45 to 50 feet. Three years later, all restrictions were removed from the pitcher's delivery, permitting for the first time an overhand motion. As of 1883, foul balls caught on the first bounce were no longer outs. A rule instituted in 1885 permitted the use of bats shaved flat on one side (a provision which lasted for eight years). Starting in 1887, the batter could no longer call for a high or a low pitch, but couldn't be called out until the fourth strike (changed back to three the next year) and was credited with a hit on a base on balls (also re-

45

scinded after one season). Probably the least effective new rule of the decade was the one introduced in 1882: "Spectators hissing or hooting at the umpire are to be promptly ejected from the grounds."

By the end of the 1880s, organized baseball was similar to what we know today. There were two recognized major leagues, with the pennant-winners of each league meeting in a post-season championship series. Minor leagues had been established throughout the country, providing instruction for younger players and a last hurrah for veterans on the downhill side of their careers. And players and owners were at war over the issues of free agency and salary caps.

WORCESTER BROWN STOCKINGS

In 1879, local boosters formed the Worcester Baseball Association and fielded a team in the minor league National Association. The club's backers launched an aggressive effort to promote the new team and bring the caliber of play up to the standards of a major league nine. They enlisted Worcester mayor Charles B. Pratt to serve as the team president, and convinced Frank Bancroft, "the prince of baseball managers," to leave New Bedford and take on the managing job.

Home field for the team was the Worcester County Agricultural Fairgrounds, a 20-acre plot bounded by Highland, Sever, Cedar, and Agricultural Streets. The site was also known as the Driving Park because it included a track for horse trotting. Rights to use the fairgrounds for the baseball season were acquired for a payment of $500.

The team struggled early in 1879, and by late May the backers gave Bancroft an ultimatum to win games or lose his job. Bancroft promptly acquired two players who were to turn the team's fortunes around: pitcher J. Lee Richmond, captain of the Brown University baseball team, and shortstop Arthur Irwin, an amateur player from Boston. Richmond and Irwin both made their professional debuts on June 2 in an exhibition game against the National League Chicago White Stockings. Richmond shocked the White Stockings—and most Worcester fans—by no-hitting the powerful Chicago squad and taking a 11–0 win in a seven-inning contest. For the rest of the season, the Worcester club continued to improve, ending the year with a respectable record of 26 wins and 31 losses, including a number of wins in matches against National League teams.

Based on its 1879 performance, Worcester was under consideration for admission to the National League. The only stumbling block was that the city didn't have the required minimum population of 75,000. This was remedied by simply "redefining" the Worcester boundary to include all residents within four miles of the city proper. With the population issue resolved, a NL franchise was awarded for the 1880 season.

The Worcester Brown Stockings of 1880 were essentially the same lineup that had performed so successfully the year before. One addition was slugger Harry Stovey, who joined George Wood, the National Association's leading hitter in 1879, and team captain Alonzo Knight in the outfield. J. Lee Richmond shuttled between Worcester and Providence, pitching for the Brown Stockings while continuing his senior year studies at Brown University. His battery mate on the Worcester squad was Charlie Bennett, one of the nineteenth century's premier catchers, whose major league career ended tragically fourteen years later when he lost both legs in a railroad accident. Art Irwin continued as the team's shortstop, where he developed into one of the league's best fielders (in 1885, Irwin also developed the forerunner of the modern fielder's mitt when he fashioned a padded glove to protect a broken finger).

One thousand fans turned out in forty-degree weather on May 1 for Opening Day at the Fairgrounds, with many of them watching the game from carriages parked around the edge of the playing field. And they got to see what they had hoped for: the Brown Stockings pounded the Troy Trojans 13–1 to win their first game as a major league team. The victory was especially sweet because Troy had been the only NL club to oppose Worcester's admission to the League. This was the first match of what was to become an intense rivalry between the two teams.

Nine days later, Worcester defeated the defending champion Providence Grays and gained sole possession of first place. The team's success was short-lived, however. A losing streak diminished interest in the team, and by the end of May, crowds of only 300 attended the games. Local enthusiasm revived strongly after J. Lee Richmond pitched his incredible perfect game on June 12.

The Worcester Brown Stockings of 1880, their first year as a National League franchise. Frank Bancroft (center) was one of the few managers of the time who had never been a professional player. Bancroft's only playing experience was as an amateur in his hometown of Lancaster, Massachusetts. In 1878 Bancroft served as manager of the New Bedford team in the International Association (baseball's first minor league). He then went on to manage seven major league clubs, more than any manager in baseball history. Among them were Worcester and the Providence Grays. *Photo courtesy of Lew Lipset.*

June 12, 1880: The Best Ball Game on Record

J. Lee Richmond, a 140-pound lefty who was an early master of the curve ball, had a strange—but spectacular—year in 1879. While still a Brown University junior, and captain of the school's baseball team, Richmond made his professional debut on June 2, with Worcester of the National Association. On that day, he faced Cap Anson's Chicago White Stockings, who were atop the National League standings. In a rain-shortened seven-inning exhibition game, Richmond earned his ten-dollar pay by pitching a no-hitter against the NL leaders; immediately after the win, Worcester signed him to a contract for $100 a month. One week later, Richmond pitched Brown to the College Championship, defeating Yale by a score of 3–2. On June 11, in his first regular season game with Worcester, Richmond threw a two-hitter and in July pitched a no-hitter against Springfield. On September 27, J. Lee Richmond made his major-league debut, pitching for Boston against the pennant-winning Providence Grays. Richmond set a record by striking out five consecutive Grays on his way to his first major-league win. He then rejoined Brown for the school's fall baseball season.

What could Richmond possibly do for an encore? In 1880, Richmond pitched for both Brown University and the Worcester Brown Stockings, now a National League franchise. On June 12, J. Lee Richmond hurled major-league baseball's first perfect game. As reported in the *Worcester Evening Gazette* the following day:

A Wonderful Ball Game

The Worcester team, by their faultless play against the Clevelands, Saturday afternoon, placed to their credit the best ball game on record. Their rivals did not secure a run; did not make a base hit; did not score a base run. In each of the nine innings of the game the Cleveland batsmen were retired in one-two-three order, not a runner ever reaching first base.

Meantime the Clevelands were playing a game no team need be ashamed of. For three innings they retired the Worcesters as fast as they came to the bat, and in the fourth, after Richmond's hit, a neat double play made almost equally short work. The fifth inning was a disastrous one, however, and the trouble was in a strange place. Irwin led off with a safe hit, Bennett was given his base on balls, and Whitney struck the ball to the pitcher. He turned and threw it to Dunlap, trusting for an easy "double" of Bennett on the "force out," and Whitney at first base. Dunlap—"old reliability Dunlap"—failed to hold the ball, and as quickly as Irwin, who was well on toward third base, saw the juggle, he passed the bag and rushed for the home plate. Dunlap secured the ball and threw it for the plate, but not to it, for it went several feet over the catcher's head, and struck the back-board with a thud just as Irwin scored, amidst wild excitement. This double error by one of the best players in the League, gave the game to the Worcesters.

Or course so faultless a game was rapidly played. It was half over in 45 minutes . . . the total time being an hour and 26 minutes, making the game one of the quickest ever played. The score has interesting points in every column:—

WORCESTERS

	A.B.	R.	B.	T.B.	P.O.	A.	E.
Wood, l f	4	0	0	0	0	0	0
Richmond, p	3	0	1	1	0	6	0
Knight, r f	3	0	0	0	1	1	0
Irwin, s s	3	1	2	2	2	3	0
Bennett, c	2	0	0	0	8	0	0
Whitney, 3b	3	0	0	0	1	2	0
Sullivan, 1b	3	0	0	0	14	0	0
Corey, c f	3	0	0	0	1	0	0
Creamer, 2b	3	0	0	0	0	4	0
Totals	27	1	3	3	27	16	0

CLEVELANDS

	A.B.	R.	1B.	T.B.	P.O.	A.	E.
Dunlap, 2b	3	0	0	0	4	2	2
Hankinson, 3b	3	0	0	0	0	0	0
Kennedy, c	3	0	0	0	6	1	0
Phillips, 1b	3	0	0	0	7	0	0
Schaffer, r f	3	0	0	0	2	0	0
McCormick, p	3	0	0	0	0	10	0
Gilligan, c f	3	0	0	0	1	0	0
Glasscock, s s	3	0	0	0	0	2	0
Hanlon, l f	3	0	0	0	1	0	0
Totals	27	0	0	0	21	15	2

Innings	1	2	3	4	5	6	7	8	9		
Worcesters	0	0	0	0	1	0	0	0	0	—	1
Clevelands	0	0	0	0	0	0	0	0	0	—	0

1st on balls, Worcesters 1; left on bases, Worcesters 3; struck out—Richmond 2, Corey 2, Sullivan, Wood, Bennett, Shaffer, Hanlon, Phillips, Glasscock; balls called, on Richmond 44, McCormick 79, strikes called, on Richmond 9, McCormick 15; douple play—Glasscock, Dunlap, and Phillips; time of game, 1 hour 26 minutes, umpire, Bradley.

The *Gazette* report goes on to reveal that Richmond had pitched the game on an empty stomach and that he was still four days away from graduation:

Richmond graduates from Brown University, Wednesday. A locomotive has been chartered to bring him from Providence to Worcester between 2 and 3 o'clock. The train on which he came up Saturday was delayed and he went on the field without his dinner.

J. Lee Richmond had a brief major-league career, using his baseball income to finance his education. While pitching for three National League teams—Boston, Worcester, and Providence—Richmond earned bachelors, masters, and medical degrees. He retired from the game in 1883, at age 26, to practice medicine.

Although interest in the team revived, the Brown Stockings foundered in the standings. Injuries and illnesses took their toll, and an eight-game losing streak in July dropped Worcester toward the league cellar. Fans were impatient with the team's lack of success and demonstrated their feelings during the games; Worcester spectators became so notorious for unruly behavior that one umpire resigned rather than officiate a game in Worcester. The good news for umpires and opponents was that crowds were again dwindling. Only one hundred fans turned out at the Fairgrounds for the final match of the season—a game in which Worcester defeated Providence to move into fifth place in the final standings, with a 40–43 record, just ahead of Boston.

The Brown Stockings suffered a serious defection at the end of the season. Manager Frank Bancroft quit the club due to disagreements with the board of directors. Bancroft went to Detroit, where he assumed the helm of the National League's newest addition, the Detroit Wolverines. Along with him, Bancroft took four of Worcester's most capable players: Charlie Bennett, Alonzo Knight, George Wood, and third-baseman Art Whitney.

To fill the voids, several veterans were acquired. Utility player Mike Dorgan came from Providence to serve as right fielder, captain, and manager. Hick Carpenter, one of the few left-handed third basemen in baseball history (oddly enough, he batted righty) was picked up from Cincinnati. Buttercup Dickerson and Pete "Monkey" Hotaling joined Dorgan in the outfield. Doc Bushong (a dental student who earned his Doctor of Dental Surgery degree the following year) had split the catching chores with Charlie Bennett in 1880, and inherited the job full-time for 1881.

Worcester again started strong, winning its first eight games of the season. On May 30, the largest home crowd in the history of the franchise turned out when Frank Bancroft and the Detroit Wolverines came to town. The fans—3,652 strong—gave the former Brown Stockings a hospitable welcome back to "The Heart of the Commonwealth," even presenting old favorite Charlie Bennett with a $150 gold watch. They were then treated to a revenge of sorts as Worcester defeated the Wolverines 8–4.

Unfortunately, after the victory over Detroit, the team again collapsed, losing thirteen of its next seventeen games. The club's management made changes hoping to turn things around: Mike Dorgan was suspended, Harry Stovey was named captain, and team treasurer Freeman Brown was appointed manager. Mayor (and team president) Charles Pratt tried a pep talk. Nothing helped. The skid continued, and Worcester ended the season in last place with a .390 winning percentage.

To the astonishment of Worcester fans, the team fared even worse in 1882. During the off-season, Dorgan and Dickerson were suspended by the National League for "crankiness" (including drunkenness and insubordination). Pitcher J. Lee Richmond was suffering from a chronic sore arm that had been overused (Richmond had led the league with 74 games pitched in 1880, and made 53 appearances in 1881). Three managers were tried: Freeman Brown began at the helm, then made way for Tommy Bond, who'd been brought in to help Richmond with the pitching duties; finally, Jack Chapman was hired to manage the final third of the season. A thirteen-game losing streak in mid-season secured the team's grip on last place in the standings.

Spectators were so sparse at home games that the club offered the first two-games-for-the-price-of-one admission in major league history on September 25 (previous doubleheaders had always been separate paid admissions). Four days later, an all-time record low attendance of *18* turned out for a game against Troy—breaking the record of 25 that had been set the day before.

Worcester ended its third and final active year in the major leagues with a dismal record of 18 wins and 66 losses. National League officials promptly announced the club's "resignation" from the league, and on December 6, 1882, Worcester officially withdrew its membership from the National League of Professional Base Ball Clubs. There was some consolation in that the Troy franchise was dropped at the same time. Both cities were awarded honorary lifetime memberships in the National League, which they still hold.

In 1992, Worcester and Troy renewed their rivalry, playing exhibition games in the National League Nostalgia Series. Games were played under 1882 rules, with players garbed in old-style uniforms. On June 20, 1992, more than 2,000 fans (including the author) turned out at Worcester's Fitton Field to see the Brown Stockings defeat the Trojans 3–1.

YALE BLUE

Harvard's long reign as the country's dominant college baseball team ended in the 1880s when Yale won a string of championships.

Until 1880, there had been no structure to determine an official "champion" team. When Brown University defeated Yale for the "college championship" in 1879, it was an informal title. To provide a regular schedule and method of determining a champion, the Intercollegiate Base Ball Association was formed in December 1879. Its members were Amherst, Brown, Dartmouth, Harvard, Princeton, and Yale. The Association also attempted to address the issue of player eligibility. The situation of J. Lee Richmond playing both professionally with Worcester and as a student for Brown University had generated opposition to the use of players who had played for professional clubs. Although Yale had been one of Richmond's victims, the New Haven college was still in favor of schools being allowed to field paid ballplayers as long as such players were also bona fide students. When the Association adopted a rule restricting eligibility to amateurs, Yale withdrew from the Association in its first year.

Member schools of the Intercollegiate Base Ball Association were required to play two games against each of the other Association colleges, and the team with the best record in these games was awarded the title of "champion." Other than these Association games, the colleges all continued to play schedules of their own choosing against school teams, professional nines, and local amateur clubs. Yale, although not formally participating in the Association in 1880, declared itself to be the champion college team in the country based on a 7–1 record against other schools and an impressive 11–2 record against professionals.

Yale rejoined the Association in 1881 and won the championship six times in seven years. The only loss during this string occurred in 1885, when Harvard experienced the best season in its history, going undefeated in Association play and posting an overall record of 27 wins with only one loss.

Yale rebounded to take the 1886 title, and making his first appearance for the Blue that season was Amos Alonzo Stagg, class of '88. Stagg went on to pitch a total of five years for Yale. With him on the mound, Yale continued its dominance of college

Above: Splendid view of college baseball action on the green in Hanover, New Hampshire. The game was played on June 26, 1882, with home team Dartmouth defeating Harvard 11–10. *Photo courtesy of Dennis Goldstein.* *Below:* One of the first organized women's baseball teams: the 1883 Mount Holyoke Nine of Mount Holyoke Female Seminary (later Mount Holyoke College) in South Hadley, Massachusetts. Although the long skirts of the uniform hindered running, they proved useful in stopping or trapping ground balls. After the school's charter was revised to establish Mt. Holyoke as a college, baseball was officially instituted as a sport in the spring of 1891. *Photo courtesy of the Mount Holyoke College Archives and Special Collections.*

Sept. 2, 1880: The Latest Yankee Notion

Two years after Thomas Edison filed his first patent for "Electric Lights," the first baseball game under artificial lights was played on Nantasket Beach in Hull, Massachusetts. The game was organized by Boston's Northern Electric Light Company to demonstrate the feasibility of lighting entire cities from clusters of electric lamps mounted on towers. The back lawn of Hull's Sea Foam House was used for the diamond. Three 100-foot high wooden towers had been constructed by Northern Electric, and a dozen lamps were atop each tower to provide the necessary illumination. The teams invited to participate in the historic experiment were picked nines from the local department stores Jordan Marsh and R. H. White. The *Boston Evening Transcript* reported the following day:

> *The game of base ball played at night by electric light, at Nantasket Beach, is the latest Yankee notion. The score, 16 to 16, shows that the playing was not bad; that is, had light enough to get on with. Still, the players complain that it was not sufficient, was too much like moonlight; so that, if the projectors of the experiment wish to convince the public that they can shed light enough over a city from elevated stands to allow people to sit in their houses and pursue their ordinary evening occupations without gas, candle or lamp light, more light still will be necessary.*

With the game locked in a 16–16 tie after nine innings, the contest was called off—but not because of darkness. Play was terminated so that the teams could catch the last boat back to Boston. Fifty-five years after the experiment on Nantasket Beach, the first night baseball game was played in the major leagues.

baseball and was especially successful against Harvard. During his time at Yale, Stagg pitched 21 successive games against Harvard, winning 15 of them.

Throughout the 1880s, colleges struggled to establish guidelines for conducting their baseball programs. Harvard President Charles Eliot was one of the most vocal forces trying to reduce the influence of professionalism on college sport and to establish eligibility guidelines. Attempts were made to prohibit the participation of students who had played professional ball, limit player eligibility to four years (some players remained on university rosters through years of graduate school), and eliminate the use of paid coaches. The strongest opposition to these reforms came from the students themselves, who protested that their own clubs would be the most damaged by such measures.

The Intercollegiate Base Ball Association disbanded before the end of the decade, to be replaced by the College League, which Yale continued to dominate.

BOSTON UNIONS

Baseball was not only the national pastime in the 1880s, but also an attractive business opportunity. Two major leagues and many more minor league and semi-pro clubs were operating, and, although not all were profitable, they demonstrated that baseball games could attract paying customers.

In September 1883, a third major league, the Union Association, was organized. One of the unique features of the new league was that it did not include the reserve clause in its contracts and refused to recognize the clause as binding players to any of the established leagues.

A record *thirty-four* major-league teams took the field in 1884—eight in the National League, thirteen in the American Association, and thirteen in the Union Association.

One of the Union Association franchises was located in Boston. The president of the Boston Unions was Frank Winslow, but George Wright also lent his name and prestige to the new team. By this time, Wright was no longer active on the diamond, instead devoting himself to his growing sporting goods company, Wright & Ditson, in Boston. It is probably no coincidence that Wright's endorsement of the Union Association coincided with that league's decision to adopt the baseball manufactured by Wright & Ditson as its official ball.

The Boston Union Association club was organized on such short notice that there wasn't enough time to build a suitable ballpark by opening day. With no better site available to them, the Dartmouth Street Baseball & Bicycle Grounds in Back Bay was used for Boston's home games. The playing field in the former racetrack was so small, that for the first two months of the season balls hit over the left field fence were ground-rule doubles.

The roster was also pieced together quickly. Tim Murnane came out of a five-year retirement to assume the dual role of first baseman and manager. Both of the team's starting pitchers were considered washed-up by the other leagues: James Burke had a record of 0–1 in two years with the National League, and former star Tommy Bond hadn't won a big-league game since 1880.

Most of the team was made up of players who hailed from the Boston area: second baseman Tom O'Brien, shortstop Walter Hackett, and the entire outfield of Kid Butler, Cannonball Crane, and Mike Slattery. Veteran Lew Brown, who had played for National League pennant winners in Boston and Providence, did most of the catching.

The Boston Unions got off to a poor start, posting a record of only 8–17 under Tim Murnane's leadership. At that point, Murnane was relieved of his managerial responsibilities and replaced by Tom Furniss, a man with no previous playing or managing experience. Furniss's reign was even briefer than Murnane's, lasting only ten games before he was fired. The Unions' third and final manager also lacked professional experience. He was twenty-four-year-old Jacob Morse, a sportswriter for the *Boston Herald* (ironically, the Unions' first manager, Tim Murnane, later became a sportswriter for the *Boston Globe*).

Under Morse's direction, the team performed well, winning 46 games and losing 28 over the rest of the season. Cannonball Crane developed into one of the league's

This 1884 Hudson, Massachusetts team includes a couple of young men from neighboring towns who went on to have extraordinary baseball careers. In the center is catcher and future Hall-of-Famer Wilbert Robinson, from Bolton. Robinson played for the legendary Baltimore Orioles of the 1890s when that team was the Boston Beaneaters' primary rival. He later managed the Brooklyn Dodgers for 18 seasons; during his tenure there, the team was called the "Robins" in his honor. Seated at the far left is outfielder Jimmy Ryan from Clinton, Massachusetts. The year after this photo was taken, Ryan began an 18-year major league career, playing in more than 2,000 games and totaling 2,500 hits with a .306 lifetime average. *Photo courtesy of the National Baseball Library & Archive, Cooperstown, N.Y.*

leading sluggers. James Burke pitched better than .500 ball, ending the season at 19–15. Tommy Bond won 13 games against 9 defeats until his arm went bad; he then left Boston to try his luck with the Indianapolis Union team (where he lost five games without a single victory). Another Hub native, Dupee Shaw, replaced Bond in the pitching rotation. Shaw jumped to the Unions from the National League, where he had been 9–18 with the Detroit Wolverines in the first part of the season; he went on to post a 21–15 record for his new team.

Boston was one of only five of the Union Association's thirteen clubs to field a team for the entire season, ending with a fourth-place finish. It was to be the team's only year of existence, for the Association folded after the 1884 season.

The Union Association's one season featured the final major-league appearances of Tommy Bond, Lew Brown, and James Burke. The year also marked one notable debut: Tommy McCarthy, another Boston native, played his first big-league game for the Boston Unions on July 10. He pitched seven games and played outfield in 48 more through the remainder of the year. Although his first season was an inauspicious one— he lost every game he pitched and batted only .215—McCarthy later became a star with the National League Boston Beaneaters, and was eventually voted into the Baseball Hall of Fame, the only veteran of the Union Association to be so honored.

WORLD CHAMPION PROVIDENCE GRAYS

After the pennant-winning season of 1879, the Grays lost most of their players as well as their manager. George Wright, who had led the '79 champions, elected to retire and devote himself to his growing sporting goods business in Boston (he later came out of retirement and made a brief return to the big leagues). Jim O'Rourke was another major loss; he also went back to Boston, to play for the Red Caps. Remaining on the roster from the 1879 club were Joe Start, Paul Hines, Tom York, and pitcher John Montgomery Ward.

Opening day of the 1880 season for the Providence Grays was May 1. A throng of almost 3,000 fans turned out at Messer Park to witness the raising of the championship pennant for the previous year. They then witnessed a 8–0 shutout over the visiting Boston club.

The team continued to play well throughout the season. John Ward, with batting support from Start and Hines, pitched the Grays to a strong second-place finish in 1880. Ward had 39 wins, led the league in shutouts, and on June 17—five days after J. Lee Richmond achieved the feat—pitched the second perfect game in major-league history.

The directors of the Providence franchise were not satisfied with finishing second, however, and determined to get some fresh young players for the '81 roster. They acquired three who promptly developed into major stars: pitcher Charley "Old Hoss" Radbourn (who was actually only twenty-six years old), third baseman Jerry Denny, and catcher Barney Gilligan, who was instrumental in Radbourn's development. All of them remained with the Grays for the last five years of the club's existence.

"Old Hoss" Radbourn made his major-league pitching debut on May 5, 1881, taking a 4–2 win over Boston. As the season progressed, he eclipsed John Montgomery Ward as the Grays' preeminent pitcher. In his first four years, Radbourn posted win totals of 25, 34, 48, and 59 games; Ward slipped to 18 wins in 1881 and never again won more than 19.

Providence played well on the field, but there was strife behind the scenes among the club's directors. Attendance was down for the second straight season, and the owners were hard-pressed financially. At one point, management lacked the funds to meet the players' payroll (the total team payroll in 1881 was $13,175, with Radbourn earning $900 a year and John Ward the highest paid at $1,700). Late in the year, amid talk of disbanding the team, club president Charles Root resigned, as did several other members of the board of directors. The management quickly reorganized under new president Dr. C. T. Gardner, and funds were raised to continue for at least one more season.

The 1884 World Champion Providence Grays. Standing (left to right): Old Hoss Radbourn, p; Charlie Sweeney, p; Miah Murray, c; Jerry Denny, 3b; Paul Hines, cf; Frank Bancroft, manager; Joe Start, 1b; Charley Bassett, utility; John Cattanach, p; Cliff Carroll, lf; Arthur Irwin, ss; Jack Farrell, 2b. Sitting (left to right): Barney Gilligan, c; Paul Radford, rf; Sandy Nava, c. Of the Grays 114 games, Radbourn pitched in 75 of them, winning 59 (the highest single-season total in baseball history). After taking the National League pennant by 10 1/2 games over second-place Boston, the Grays swept the American Association champion New York Metropolitans three games to none in a postseason series to determine the "Champions of the World." *Photo courtesy of Transcendental Graphics*

After another second-place finish in 1881, venerable Harry Wright was hired to manage Providence in 1882. Under Wright's direction, the Grays were in first place on June 17 when George Wright made a highly-publicized return to the team (a major factor in coaxing the younger Wright brother back to Providence was to bolster sagging attendance). Tom York resigned the captaincy in favor of Wright, who played 46 games at shortstop for the Grays through the remainder of the season.

Providence held first place until September 17, but then suffered a losing streak that killed the team's chances for the championship. For the third year in a row, the Grays ended up second to Cap Anson's pennant-winning Chicago White Stockings.

The Grays did play a three-game postseason series against Boston for the "championship of New England." The Red Caps won the first game of the series, but John Ward and Hoss Radbourn pitched shutouts in the next two matches to give Providence the regional title.

Aug. 17, 1882: Two Games in One

In 1882, a pitcher was expected to be a full-time, all-purpose ballplayer. The Providence Grays that year had two pitchers sharing mound duties: John Montgomery Ward and Old Hoss Radbourn. Both Ward and Radbourn played in all but one of the team's games that season; when one of them was pitching, the other was in the outfield. Relief pitching appearances were a rarity (John Ward led the league in saves that season with 1), so when Ward and Detroit's Stump Weidman hooked up in an 18-inning marathon pitching dual, it was no surprise that both hurlers went the duration. The *Providence Journal* reported on the game:

A DOUBLE GAME
PROVIDENCE SCORES A VICTORY OF VICTORIES

"Two games in one" is what the eighth Providence-Detroit game, played at Messer Park, yesterday afternoon, might appropriately be termed, in that it required eighteen innings to determine the victory by the attainment of a single tally—a contest unsurpassed in the history of the League in length, and in the wonderfully brilliant fielding which was performed by the diamond knights, as also clever and steady pitching during nearly three hours of continuous exercise. Ward and Weidman occupied the points, and a glance at the batting columns is a suggestive commentary upon the strategy and coolness which characterized their manipulation of the sphere, yet they were batted freely into the diamond, and there received magnificent support as well as behind the bat. One singular feature of the game lies in the fact that the same number of men reached first base and were left on both sides, and Detroit sent but one man less to bat, which shows how uniform was the play of the teams.

Since 1882 rules only allowed substitutions in the event of injury or illness, only nine players were used by each team for the duration of the contest. The game didn't end until Old Hoss Radbourn, playing outfield on this day, broke the scoreless deadlock with one swing of his bat. As the *Journal* reporter put it:

Radbourn was the first batsman for Providence in the eighteenth inning, and catching the sphere fairly on his bat he drove it high over the left field fence for a home run, and rounding the bases, earned the winning talley [sic] mid tremendous excitement.

During the marathon game, a crowd gathered in the Providence neighborhood of Turk's Head where the *Providence Journal* office was located. The newspaper posted inning-by-inning updates in the front window:

> *The JOURNAL bulletin was anxiously watched by hundreds of citizens assembled on Turk's Head, and the glorious announcement was received with deafening applause. The teams take a rest today and close the series on Saturday. The score:*

PROVIDENCE

	Batting			Running			Fielding		
	A.B.	1B.	T.B.	R.	RB.	L.	P.O.	A.	E.
Hines, c f	7	1	1	0	1	1	1	1	0
Farrell, 2b	7	1	1	0	1	1	6	9	0
Start, 1b	7	0	0	0	0	0	26	0	1
Ward, p	7	1	1	0	1	1	0	5	0
York, l f	7	1	1	0	1	1	3	0	0
Radbourn, r f	7	1	4	1	1	0	1	0	0
Wright, s s	6	1	3	0	2	1	2	5	1
Denny, 3b	6	1	1	0	2	1	5	11	1
Nava, c	6	0	0	0	2	2	9	1	2
Totals	60	7	12	1	11	8*53		32	5

DETROIT

	Batting			Running			Fielding		
	A.B.	1B.	T.B.	R.	RB.	L.	P.O.	A.	E.
Wood, l f	7	1	1	0	1	1	3	1	0
Hanlon, c f	7	1	1	0	2	1	5	0	0
Powell, 1b	7	1	1	0	1	1	21	0	1
Bennett, 3b	7	1	2	0	1	1	3	3	2
Trott, c	7	2	2	0	1	1	13	1	2
Knight, r f	6	0	0	0	2	1	1	1	0
Weidman, p	6	1	2	0	1	1	2	9	0
Whitney, s s	6	2	2	0	2	1	1	10	3
Foster, 2b	6	0	0	0	0	0	2	4	1
Totals	33	9	11	0	11	8	51	29	9

* *Knight out for running out of base line.*

INNINGS

	1	2	3	4	5	6	7	8	9	10	11	12	13	14	15	16	17	18	
Providence	0	0	0	0	0	0	0	0	0	0	0	0	0	0	0	0	1	—	1
Detroit	0	0	0	0	0	0	0	0	0	0	0	0	0	0	0	0	0	—	0

> *Umpire—Bradley. Runs earned—Providence, 1. Home run—Radbourn. Three base hit—Wright. Two base hits—Bennett, Weidman. Struck out—Providence, 6; Detroit, 4. Base on called balls—Knight. First base on errors—Providence 3; Detroit 2. Double plays—Farrell-Start (2), Denny-Farrell-Start. Passed ball—Trott. Time—2h, 40m.*

This game was one of John Ward's final moments of glory with the Providence Grays. With Old Hoss Radbourn assuming the number one pitching role, Ward left the team at the end of the season.

The Ward-Weidman duel remained the longest game on record until July 4, 1905, when Cy Young and Rube Waddell hooked up in a twenty-inning contest in Boston's Huntington Avenue Grounds. In that game, too, both pitchers went the distance and it also was won by a pitcher, with Rube Waddell driving home the winning run.

Providence signed two teams to contracts for the 1883 season. One was the established line-up, again under the management of Harry Wright. The other was a team comprised of talented local prospects dubbed the Providence Reserves. Essentially a farm club of the Grays, the Reserves were given instruction, playing time in exhibition games and modest salaries. This experiment in grooming young players was a successful one; during the season, several of the Reserves substituted in league games for injured regulars, and some went on to major-league careers.

John Montgomery Ward left Providence after the 1882 season, but two new pitchers were added to the roster. One was Charlie Sweeney, a hard-throwing twenty-year-old who some thought would prove to be as good as Old Hoss Radbourn. The other was J. Lee Richmond, who was signed after the Worcester Brown Stockings folded.

Also picked up from the defunct Worcester club was Art Irwin, who took over at shortstop from the retired George Wright. Replacing popular five-year Providence veteran Tom York in the outfield was Cliff Carroll, one of the finest fielders in the game.

The Grays again started the season strong, and again spent much of the year in first place. The only conflicts involved the pitching staff. Radbourn wanted to pitch every game, and Charlie Sweeney and J. Lee Richmond were given few chances on the mound. The team's directors felt that a three-man rotation was an unnecessary expenditure, and that two pitchers on the roster were more than enough. The club did keep Sweeney and Richmond, but Radbourn got his way, pitching in a league-leading 76 games while Sweeney was given only 20 appearances and Richmond a mere dozen.

After a hard-fought, four-way battle for the pennant, the Grays ended in third place, losing the pennant to their rivals from Boston.

The playing of the 1883 team was solid enough that management did not try to change the roster for the following season. The only important change was at the helm, with Frank Bancroft assuming the managerial reins from Harry Wright.

1884 turned out to be an historic season for the Providence Grays and for baseball. Opening Day at Messer Park was a disappointment, both because the Grays lost and because attendance was less than half the park's capacity. There was also a furor among fans because the team had adopted a new uniform: replacing the famous "Providence gray" were drab outfits with blue trimmings. The change in uniform style seemed to change the team's fortunes, however. After the opening loss, the Grays won nine of their next ten games, and by June first were at the top of the standings. Charlie Sweeney, as the team's second pitcher, showed signs of proving the earlier predictions of greatness. On June 7, Sweeney set a major-league record by striking out 19 Boston batters in a nine-inning game (a record that lasted for more than a century, until it was broken by Boston Red Sox pitcher Roger Clemens). Although Sweeney possessed a world of talent, he also had a hot temper and a drinking problem. A month after setting his strikeout record, a hung-over Sweeney argued with manager Frank Bancroft during a game, and the pitcher ended the argument by walking off the field. Under the rules of the day, Providence had to finish playing the game with only eight men, and lost the game. Charlie Sweeney, with a 17–8 record, was immediately expelled from the Grays

Opening Day, 1886. The National League Boston Beaneaters and New York Giants pose for their picture. After the Providence Grays finished the 1885 season 33 games out of first place, their stockholders sold the club—players included—to Boston. The prize acquisition for the Beaneaters was pitcher Old Hoss Radbourn, who had averaged *45* wins a season in his last three years with the Grays. Radbourn (back row, far left) is shown here with his new team. Judging from his gesture, he was not entirely happy about the change. *Photo courtesy of the Library of Congress.*

and the National League (he promptly signed with the Union Association, where he won 24 more games, for a season total of 41 victories).

After Sweeney's departure, Radbourn pitched nearly all of the team's remaining games. He appeared in a total of 75 games in 1884, and set an all-time record by winning *59* of them. Among his victories was a memorable contest against Boston that was later described as "one of the greatest ever played on the old South End grounds." The game took place on August 9, with Radbourn matched up against Charlie Buffinton, who was on his way to winning 48 games for Boston. The two pitchers hurled shutout ball against each other for ten full innings. Radbourn gave up only two hits and walked one batter; Buffinton yielded three hits and no walks. The duel ended in the eleventh inning, when Art Irwin hit a fly ball that passed through a hole in the rickety outfield fence of Boston's South End Grounds; the hit was ruled a home run, and Providence came away with the win.

After easily taking the National League pennant, the Grays then faced the New York Metropolitans, champions of the American Association, in a three-game series to

April 23, 1884: The Best Battery Ever Seen

On September 19, 1883, a couple of amateur town teams from East Brookfield and North Brookfield played a match for the title "Champions of Central Massachusetts" and a silver bat trophy. Behind the strong pitching of big Bill Hogan, East Brookfield won the game, and professional ballclubs started to seek Hogan's services. When the Connecticut State League was formed in 1884, the Meriden entry offered Hogan a contract to pitch for them. The East Brookfield pitcher agreed on the condition that his catcher also be accepted on the team. Hogan made the demand as a favor to his friend, whom he knew was trying to find a way out of his job in a shoe factory. Although the catcher had already been turned down for the team, Meriden agreed to give him another tryout in a preseason game against Yale. The *Meriden Daily Republican* announced on April 23, 1884:

> Connie Mack of East Brookfield, Mass., who caught Hogan for five seasons, has been engaged by the Meridens and is playing this afternoon. He is said to be a good man.

The following day, the paper reported the outcome of the game:

HOGAN'S WONDERFUL SKILL
His Deceptive Curves Too Much for The Yale Boys

> The Meriden league nine made its first appearance, Tuesday, in a regular game, and defeated the strong Yale freshman nine 8 to 4. That there was great interest taken in the club was shown by the large attendance. Every one wanted to see how the Meridens would "show up," and after the game there was general approval. With one or two changes the nine will be a very strong one—a credit to the town, and a money making investment to the stock holders, for it will be liberally patronized. Hogan and Mack proved themselves to be first class men, and it was said by many that they were the best battery ever seen on the grounds, outside of a league nine. Hogan struck out 17 of the 21 who were put out in the seven innings played, and only one base hit was made of him. That is a record that is rarely equalled. Mack caught him in a manner that was entirely satisfactory. Both received the highest praise, and they deserved it.
> The Yales gave up the contest after the seventh inning, because their catcher was broken up. As has been stated, with one or two changes the Meridens will have a big team. Massicott umpired well, as he generally does. Below is the detailed score:

MERIDENS	R.	BH.	PO.	A.	E.
Pettit, 1b	1	1	5	0	0
Campana, l.f.	2	1	0	0	0
Mack, c	1	2	11	3	1
Fitzpatrick, c.f.	0	0	0	0	0
O'Toole, 3b	0	0	4	1	1
Fay, r.f.	1	0	0	0	2
Hogan, p	2	2	1	18	6
Shaw, ss	0	0	0	1	1
Lane, 2b	1	0	1	1	1
Totals	8	6	21	24	12

YALE '87	R.	BH.	PO.	A.	E.
Ayre, c	1	1	11	1	3
Marsh, 2b	1	0	1	2	1
Tuttle, 3b	1	0	1	1	2
Brigham, 1b	0	0	7	2	1
Sheppard, c.f.	0	0	0	0	1
Gordon, p	0	0	0	8	1
Sprague, ss	1	0	0	2	0
Bayne, l.f	0	0	1	0	0
Corwin, r.f.	0	0	0	0	0
Totals	4	1	21	16	9

Innings	1	2	3	4	5	6	7		
Meridens	2	1	0	0	0	1	4	—	8
Yales	3	0	0	0	0	1	0	—	4

Balls called—on Gordon 56; on Hogan 105; struck out, Hogan 17; Gordon 5; bases on balls, Gordon 1; Hogan 6; earned runs 0; time of game, 2 hours and 13 minutes. Umpire, Massicott.

(Note: the published box score shows 22 putouts in the total for Meriden.)

The paper sung the praises of Meriden's new battery:

> *Mack and Hogan have established themselves as favorites. They play ball for all that's out and mind their own business. If East Brookfield has any more players like Mack and Hogan, let's have 'em.*

It also had a suggestion for improving the park:

> *A wire screen should be put in front of the grand stand. It don't obstruct the view and will save sore heads and broken noses.*

The game against Yale marked Connie Mack's first appearance with a professional baseball team. Immediately after the game, he was signed to a contract for $90 a month. Tragically, Bill Hogan fell ill with "galloping consumption" (tuberculosis) and died in mid-season. Connie Mack married Hogan's sister Margaret, and went on to have a 66-year career in professional baseball, including half a century as owner and manager of the Philadelphia Athletics.

determine the "Champions of the World." All of the games were played in New York's Polo Grounds, and all three were won by Old Hoss Radbourn, as Providence outscored the "Mets" 21 to 3 over the course of the three games. The final contest was played on October 25. On that day, the Providence Grays completed their sweep to win baseball's first World Series.

The team's fortunes plummeted the following year. Although there were few changes to the roster, the team simply failed to perform up to expectations. As the Grays dropped in the standings, attendance fell at Messer Park, and the club's always shaky financial situation became desperate.

The final game of the 1885 season was played on October 10, and it was to be the last major-league game played by a Providence team. The Grays finished in fourth place, a distant thirty-three games behind Chicago. The club's directors promptly sold the players to Boston and folded operations after eight years as a National League franchise.

NEW ENGLAND LEAGUES

The expansion of minor league baseball in the 1880s was even more chaotic than the changes in the major leagues. Dozens of associations formed, and most of them dissolved—often after being in business for less than a year. Strong franchises jumped from league to league, and weak ones folded.

Most of the new organizations consisted of teams scattered over broad regions of the country. During the first three seasons of the Eastern League, founded in 1884 and one of the strongest minor leagues, franchises were located all the way from Virginia to Rhode Island. Among the New England cities represented in the Eastern League were Waterbury, Bridgeport, Meriden, and Providence.

The Connecticut State League in which Connie Mack made his professional debut was one of the first minor leagues comprised solely of New England teams (although its name implied that it was limited to the Nutmeg State, the league also included teams from Holyoke and Springfield, Massachusetts). It lasted only one year.

Two New England leagues formed in 1885. One was the Southern New England League, which included teams from the defunct Connecticut State League as well as several that jumped from the Eastern League. Among the Southern New England League franchises were Bridgeport, Waterbury, and Hartford (which included Connie Mack on its roster).

Clubs from six cities in Maine and Massachusetts formed the Eastern New England League. This marked the first entry of teams from Maine—Biddeford and Portland—into organized baseball. The Massachusetts franchises were Brockton, Gloucester, Haverhill, and Lawrence. The Gloucester team folded before the season got under way. Lawrence, which ended up playing most of its home games in Manchester, New Hampshire, took the championship by winning a three-game playoff with Brockton.

The Southern New England League folded after one season, so the Eastern New England League reorganized without the "Eastern" in its name. The teams that formed the 1886 New England League were Portland (which won the championship), Brockton,

1880s baseball game in progress at Bates College in Lewiston, Maine. Note the stance of the catcher. The umpire (standing more than ten feet behind the plate) is leaning on a cane or bat, which may have served to discourage arguments from the players. From 1873 to 1880, Bates College reigned as state college champions. In 1879 Bates took the Maine amateur championship, a title that had previously gone to such established powerhouses as the Augusta Reds and Portland Resolutes. *Photo courtesy of Transcendental Graphics.*

Haverhill, Lynn, Lawrence, and the Boston Blues (one of the rare instances of a city having major league and minor league franchises at the same time).

Brockton dropped out of the New England League before the start of the 1887 season, and Lowell, Manchester, and Salem were added to the circuit. Boston and Salem dropped out of the troubled league in July, and the new Lowell club won the pennant. The next year the league consisted of Lowell (which repeated as champions), Lynn, Manchester, Portland, Salem, and Worcester. Portland folded two months into the schedule, but had the distinction of lasting the longest of the New England League's original members. The entire league ceased operation at the end of the season; when it revived two years later, Portland was back in the league and strong enough to win the 1891 pennant.

Aug. 9, 1886: What Perseverance and Pluck Can Do

The first Maine team to win a championship in organized baseball was the Portland entry of the 1886 New England League. The club moved into first place on August 9, and never relinquished the top spot. The *Portland Eastern Argus* (still referring to the league as the *Eastern* New England League) reported on the decisive victory over Newburyport, Massachusetts, that moved Portland to the top of the standings:

GOT THERE
The Portlands at the Head of the League
Which Shows What Perseverance and Pluck Can Do

The Portlands have reached the point which they have been aiming at for a long time, and now stand at the head of the Eastern New England League. In the game to-day Lovett and Whiteley were both batted out of the box, while McKinley held the Newburyports down to only two runs. The Portland boys did some heavy batting. They should receive a royal welcome on their return home Wednesday night. It was one of the easiest victories they have yet won. The score:

PORTLANDS

	AB.	R.	1B.	TB.	PO.	A.	E.
Galligan, lf	5	2	2	2	2	0	0
Kearns, 2b	6	4	5	7	3	1	1
Wheelock, ss	5	2	3	3	2	2	0
Hatfield, 3b	6	2	3	5	0	0	0
Sheffler, cf	6	3	3	5	1	0	0
O'Rourke, c	5	1	1	1	8	0	0
Reilly, rf	5	1	1	1	0	0	2
Shoeneck, 1b	5	1	1	2	11	0	0
McKinley, p	5	1	0	0	0	12	3
Totals	48	17	19	26	27	15	6

NEWBURYPORTS

	AB.	R.	1B.	TB.	PO.	A.	E.
Murphy, ss,c	4	0	1	1	1	1	0
LaRoque, 2b	4	0	1	1	1	1	1
Flannagan, 1b	4	0	0	0	12	0	2
Whiteley, lf&p	4	0	0	0	1	4	0
Wilson, c,ss	3	1	2	3	4	1	0
O'Brien, rf	4	1	1	2	2	0	1
Cull, 3b	4	0	0	0	4	4	2
Lovett, p&lf	4	0	0	0	1	6	2
Gruber, cf	3	0	1	1	1	0	1
Totals	34	2	6	8	27	17	9

Innings	1	2	3	4	5	6	7	8	9		
Portlands	0	1	0	7	0	4	3	0	2	—	17
Newburyports	0	2	0	0	0	0	0	0	0	—	2

Earned runs, Portlands 2. Bases stolen, Sheffler, Reilly, O'Brien, Larouque, Wilson. Two-base hits, Kearns 2, Schoneck, Wilson, O'Brien. Three hits, Hatfield, Sheffler. Passed balls, Wilson 3, Murphy 1. Wild pitches, Lovett 3, Whitely 1. First base on balls, Portlands 2, Newburyports 2. First base on errors, Portlands 6, Newburyports 2. Struck out, Lovett 4, McKinley 5. Double plays, Cull, Larouque and Flannagan. Left on bases, Portlands 6, Newburyports 7. Umpire, Freligh. Time, 2h., 5m.

(Box score note: the published box score is inconsistent in the spelling of players' names.)

> The biggest star of the Portland club was Kid Madden, a diminutive 19-year-old local boy from the Munjoy Hill section of the city. The year after leading Portland to the New England League pennant, Madden was pitching in the National League, where he won 21 games in his rookie season with Boston. Madden wasn't the only one in the 1886 Portland roster to go on to the big leagues—the entire starting line-up went on to have major-league careers. The team was so strong, that they took on the Boston Beaneaters after the regular season, and behind Madden's pitching beat the National Leaguers 7–4. The *Eastern Argus* declared that "the Portlands can justly lay claim to the championship of New England."

Vermont was the last New England state to field a team in a professional baseball league. The North Eastern League organized in 1887 with clubs in Burlington, Montpelier, Rutland, and St. Albans. The league got off to a late start, with a schedule beginning in July, but finished early, as Burlington, Montpelier, and Rutland folded, leaving St. Albans to take the "championship" in the North Eastern League's only year of existence.

Two more New England leagues began operations in 1888: the New England Inter-State League and another Connecticut State League, both of which lasted only one season. A Rhode Island League formed in 1889 and proved to be one of the more successful state leagues, continuing for three years.

BLACK PLAYERS IN NEW ENGLAND

Segregation in baseball was instituted early, while the sport was still in its amateur era. In 1867, the National Association of Base Ball Players rejected the membership application of the all-black Pythian Club of Philadelphia, and established a prohibition against "the admission of any club which may be composed of one or more colored persons." This was a rare instance of the color line being spelled out in writing; the professional leagues that later barred African-American players did so under an unwritten "gentleman's agreement."

The coming of professionalism and organized leagues resulted in pressure on teams to field the best possible lineups, however, and some defied the race barrier to sign black players. More than 70 African-Americans played in organized baseball in the nineteenth century.

New England fans were treated—briefly—to seeing some of the best players in history. Moses Fleetwood Walker, who in 1884 became the first black to break into the major leagues with Toledo in the American Association, caught for Waterbury, Connecticut in the Eastern League and Southern New England League from 1885 to 1886. Second baseman Frank Grant, considered by many historians to be the best black player of the nineteenth century, played for the 1886 Meriden, Connecticut entry in the Eastern League. Pioneer Bud Fowler was second baseman of the Montpelier, Ver-

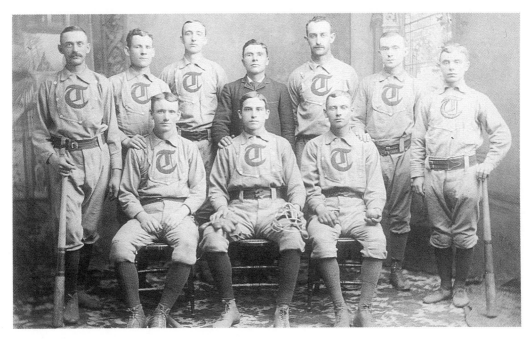

The Fall River Tecumsehs, organized in 1883, were champions of the city four years later. The earliest Fall River baseball teams on record were the Anawans and Quequechans of the mid-1860s. The Quequechans remained a leading team for twenty years, taking the city championship away from the Tecumsehs in 1888. *Photo courtesy of Transcendental Graphics.*

mont team in the 1887 North Eastern League. George Stovey, probably the best African-American pitcher of the century, starred for Worcester in the New England League in 1888, one year after setting the International League record for most wins in a season with 34 (a record which still stands).

Those African-American players who were able to break in with white teams had no easy time of it on the playing field. Racist teammates sabotaged them, with white pitchers refusing to take signals from black catchers, and fielders committing intentional errors behind black pitchers (there are few photographs of integrated teams because white players often refused to sit for pictures with black teammates). White opponents were even worse: pitchers used the heads of African-American players as targets for their fastballs, and base runners went out of their way to plant their spikes in the legs of black infielders. Long before catchers started using shin guards, Frank Grant and Bud Fowler wore wooden shin protectors to shield themselves from cleats when playing second base.

In 1887, some of the country's leading African-American teams formed a league of their own: the League of Colored Base Ball Clubs, commonly known as "the Colored League." One of the league's six founding teams was the Boston Resolutes, managed by A. A. Seldon and Marshall Thompson, and starring William Seldon, one of the best pitchers of the era.

Remarkably, the League of Colored Base Ball Clubs was admitted into organized

Among the earliest Vermont teams was the Norwich University baseball club, organized in June of 1870. This 1887 team was the "Vermont College Champions," beating out rivals Middlebury College and the University of Vermont. *Photo courtesy of Norwich University Special Collections.*

baseball as a signatory to the National Agreement. The league began play on May 6, 1887, but its member teams were so underfinanced that it folded in only thirteen days. After defeating the Falls City team in Louisville, the Boston Resolutes were stranded in Kentucky without enough money to return to Boston. The Resolutes players had to work odd jobs to make their way back home. They could enjoy some small consolation in that they were champions of the short-lived league. Boston's win over Louisville had given the Resolutes a perfect 1–0 record. That one game played by the Resolutes in the League of Colored Base Ball Clubs was the only one ever to be played by a New England team in an organized black baseball league.

HARD TIMES FOR THE BEANEATERS

After winning six championships in the nine years from 1871 through 1879, Boston slumped badly in the 1880s, taking only one title during the decade. The team's consecutive sixth-place finishes (in an eight-team league) in 1880 and 1881 resulted in manager Harry Wright being fired by club president Arthur Soden.

Arthur Soden, the most prominent member of a triumvirate that ran the Boston National League franchise for more than twenty years, was himself responsible for some of the team's problems. In an age when owners were cast from the robber baron mold,

Soden was worse than most. His stated philosophy was that "baseball is conducted primarily to make money," and he cut costs ruthlessly. Player morale suffered as Soden slashed salaries, reduced meal allowances, housed the team in the fleabag hotels, and charged players' wives full admission to games. Attendance dropped at South End Grounds in part because it was the worst maintained ballpark in the major leagues. And, although the park was rarely filled to capacity anyway, Soden antagonized Boston sportswriters by ripping out the press box to install additional seats for paying spectators.

There were several key departures from the roster that had won the 1878 pennant. George Wright played a total of only eight games for Boston in 1880 and 1881, and the 1880 season was Jim O'Rourke's last one with the Red Caps. Also gone was pitcher Tommy Bond, who had won forty games a season from 1877 to 1879. Bond slipped to a 26-29 record in 1880, and retired from the game after losing his first three decisions in 1881. He became a coach at Harvard, and instructed a couple of young pitchers from the Boston area who went on to Hall of Fame careers: John Clarkson and Tim Keefe. Bond attempted a major-league comeback with the Boston Unions in 1884, and made his final professional appearance two years later with the Brockton club of the New England League.

Taking Tommy Bond's place as the team's number one starter was Grasshopper Jim Whitney, a lanky right-hander who in his rookie season of 1881 led the National League in wins with 31.

Upon Harry Wright's dismissal after the 1881 season, first baseman "Honest John" Morrill was appointed manager. Morrill, a Boston native popular with the fans, was the last remaining member of the city's original 1876 Red Caps. Under Morrill, with Whitney and veteran Bobby Matthews sharing the pitching chores, Boston finished 1882 in a tie for third place. During the 1882 season, National League founder William Hulbert died, and Boston owner Arthur Soden was selected to serve as league president for the balance of the year (although Soden had few friends among players or fans, he apparently had the respect of his fellow owners).

At the start of the 1883 season, Morrill relinquished the managing job to second baseman Black Jack Burdock, but again took over the helm in mid-season. Jim Whitney remained the team's number one pitcher, winning 37 games and leading the league in strikeouts with 345. The club's second pitcher was Charlie Buffinton, the pride of Fall River, Massachusetts, who had broken in with Boston the year before. Buffinton quickly developed into one of the best pitchers in the league, posting a record of 25–14 in his first full season. Behind the pitching of Whitney and Buffinton, Boston upset the favored Chicago and Providence teams to win the 1883 National League pennant— the only title Boston would take in the decade. It was around this time that the franchise began to be known as the "Beaneaters," a nickname that would last for twenty years. After a second-place finish in 1884, the team again went into a slump for several years.

Arthur Soden finally began to invest some money in his ball club. At the close of the 1885 season, Boston bought out the Providence Grays primarily to obtain pitcher Old Hoss Radbourn. After the 1886 season, Soden shelled out $10,000—an

1888 lithograph of Boston's second South End Grounds, situated at the corner of Walpole Street and Columbus Avenue. The park that had been home to the National Association Red Stockings and National League Red Caps from 1871 to 1887 was torn down at the end of the 1887 season. When the new South End Grounds opened on May 25, 1888, it was the most splendid in baseball, with a double-decked grandstand and a seating capacity of almost 7,000. *Photo courtesy of the Boston Public Library, Print Department.*

unprecedented sum—to buy flamboyant star Michael "King" Kelly from Chicago. A year later, Soden paid another $10,000 for pitcher John Clarkson.

In addition to acquiring players, Soden undertook to build a baseball palace for them to play in. On May 25, 1888, the rebuilt South End Grounds opened to a crowd of approximately 7,000 Boston fans. The magnificent new park had a double-decked grandstand called the Grand Pavilion. Elaborately carved columns supported the upper deck, and six spires rose above the grandstand roof, with pennants flying from the spires.

The only thing Boston didn't get in 1888 was the championship, finishing a disappointing fourth. The season marked Morrill's last as the Beaneaters' manager. Since 1878, Boston's infield had included John Morrill at first base, Jack Burdock at second, and Ezra Sutton at third. After eleven years together, all three were let go at the conclusion of the 1888 season.

Arthur Soden went shopping for another player and picked up one of the greatest sluggers of the nineteenth century: "Big Dan" Brouthers. With Brouthers, the 1889 Boston Beaneaters now had four future Hall-of-Famers on the team, all of whom contributed to a spectacular season. John Clarkson led the league in wins (47), shut-outs, and strikeouts. Old Hoss Radbourn contributed 20 wins. Dan Brouthers took over the first base position and won the league batting title with a .373 average. King Kelly, primarily used in right field, led the league in doubles and stole 68 bases.

Under new manager Jim Hart (who three years later would become president of the Chicago club), Boston won 83 games in 1889, tying New York for the most victories. The Beaneaters had to settle for second place, however, because they had played and lost two more games than the Giants.

Although the team failed to win a second National League title in the decade, the seeds had been planted for what was to become a dynasty in the 1890s.

4

1890–1899:
Playing Hardball

By the 1890s, there were few vestiges left of the gentlemanly courtesies that had typi-fied the game in the 1850s. Baseball had gone from sport to open warfare, with battles fought in board rooms as well as on playing fields.

The decade opened with a players' rebellion. There were once again three major leagues in 1890 as the Players' League, under control of the ballplayers themselves, competed with the American Association and the National League. The attempt by the players to run their own league was called the "Brotherhood War" and the National League established a "War Committee" to combat the Brotherhood of Professional Base Ball Players. The National League emerged victorious over the Players' League, which folded after one season. The American Association collapsed a year later, giving the National League a monopoly which lasted from 1892 to 1900.

The warfare on the field was just as intense, and more direct, with spikes, bats, and balls used as weapons. Three teams dominated baseball in the 1890s: the Baltimore Orioles, the Cleveland Spiders, and the Boston Beaneaters—none of which were known for their genteel deportment on the field. Oliver "Patsy" Tebeau, the manager and first baseman of the Spiders through most of the decade, expressed the attitude of the era when he declared, "A milk-and-water, goody-goody player can't wear a Cleveland uniform."

Typically, only one umpire officiated a game, and he was unable to see everything at once. Players took advantage of the situation by tripping opposing base runners, flashing mirrors into the eyes of batters, stashing extra baseballs in high outfield grass, and holding the belts of runners attempting to tag up on fly balls.

Regulations intended to help umpires control the games were added to the rulebook. In 1895, umpires were authorized to fine players $25 to $100 for misconduct. The next year, the range of fines was lowered to a mere $5 to $10; however, players guilty of "indecent or vulgar language" were subject to ejection from the game and a $25 fine. In 1897, a rule against obstruction—in which a fielder blocks the path of a base runner—was added. These rules had little effect on players like Baltimore's John McGraw or Cleveland's Patsy Tebeau or Boston's Tommy Tucker. Nor did they deter violent "cranks" (as fans were then called) who threw beer glasses at players on the field, and stoned opposing teams as they traveled in horse-drawn carriages between their hotel and ballpark (in one such incident, the Beaneaters' Kid Nichols and Hugh Duffy were injured when a Pittsburgh mob stoned them after Boston defeated the home town team to win the 1893 championship).

With inadequate protection from the rulebook or league officials, umpires occasionally took matters into their own hands. Legendary umpire Tim Hurst once had eight Cleveland players arrested during a game; another time, he drew a pistol from his belt and fired into the air to quell a violent crowd.

One rule change that did have a lasting effect was instituted in 1893. Pitchers no longer were positioned within a box; from that year on, they instead threw from a rubber slab located sixty feet, six inches from home plate. Many baseball historians date the start of the "modern era" at this point.

The first years of the modern era were troubled ones, however. Rowdyism on the field and in the stands kept many spectators away, as did the prospect of fire—in 1894 alone, there were ballpark fires in Boston, Baltimore, Chicago, and Philadelphia, and more than twenty parks burned down during the decade. A monopoly by the National League, which was comprised of twelve teams, also diminished fan interest. Local minor leagues were gaining strength and attention, but at the major-league level, attendance was dropping and many clubs were losing money. It was clear by the end of the decade that fundamental changes were needed to regain public support for big-league baseball.

REBELS IN BOSTON

Under the leadership of former Providence pitching star John Montgomery Ward, the Brotherhood of Professional Base Ball Players organized in 1885, partly in response to a $2,000 salary cap instituted by National League owners. A year later, every major-league city had a Brotherhood chapter, and more than one hundred big-leaguers were members. The players initially sought to abolish the hated reserve rule. Later, they aimed for more modest goals that included requiring owners to abide by contracts and giving players a say in any transactions that would send them to another team.

The National League was particularly antagonistic to the players' organization and refused to cooperate with it. For the 1889 season, the owners unveiled a new scheme called the "Classification Plan." According to the plan, each player would be graded by his manager and owner, and placed in one of five categories from "A" to "E." There was a salary limit for each class of player, and, in addition, low-ranked players could be required to perform tasks such as sweeping the ballpark or working the ticket booths. Players were given the choice of either going along with the scheme or being blacklisted by organized baseball. When the National League refused even to meet with a committee representing the Brotherhood, the players decided to take action: they formed a league of their own.

Brotherhood president John Ward, an articulate, intelligent man with a law degree from Columbia University, was the driving force behind the establishment of "The Players' National League," commonly called the Players' League. There was no reserve rule in the new league, and players and investors shared power. With eight franchises,

The Boston team that won the 1890 Players League championship. In the center of the photograph is the team's manager, Mike "King" Kelly. Most of the roster had been with the National League Beaneaters the year before, including Kelly, Dan Brouthers, Old Hoss Radbourn, Billy Nash, Joe Quinn, Hardy Robinson, Kid Madden, and Tom Brown. *Photo courtesy of the National Baseball Library & Archive, Cooperstown, N.Y.*

the Players' League began operation in 1890, directly competing against the National League in seven cities, including Boston.

Most of the better players in the American Association and National League readily jumped to the Brotherhood teams. The Boston Beaneaters lineup was decimated as King Kelly, Big Dan Brouthers, Old Hoss Radbourn, Billy Nash, Joe Quinn, Hardy Richardson, Kid Madden, and Tom Brown all left the club to join the new Boston Reds in the Players' League. They were optimistic that the fans would follow them; Dan Brouthers, referring to the three businessmen who owned the Beaneaters, summed up the attitude of many of his teammates when he said, "No one would pay a nickel to see Arthur Soden play first, [William] Conant at second, and [J. B.] Billings at third." The only starting players who remained with the National League Boston team were pitcher John Clarkson and catcher Charlie Bennett.

The Boston Reds opened their home season on April 19 at the cozy Congress Street Grounds in South Boston. From the beginning, the Reds received strong support from Boston fans and favorable coverage from local newspapers. Sportswriters Jacob

Morse, of the *Boston Herald*, and Tim Murnane, of the *Boston Globe*, were among the few in the country who sided with the players in the Brotherhood War.

The Reds fielded a superb team. King Kelly managed the "rebels," in addition to filling in at catcher, shortstop, and outfield; he even pitched and won a game. The infield included slugger Dan Brouthers at first base; fine-fielding, Australian-born second baseman Joe Quinn; shortstop Art Irwin, who had starred with Worcester and Providence, and returned to New England to join the Reds; and popular third baseman Billy Nash, who had held down the position for the Beaneaters for the previous five years. In the outfield were Hardy Richardson, Tom Brown, and speedy Harry Stovey, who had led the American Association in hits, home runs, and RBIs the year before. Old Hoss Radbourn and Ad Gumbert did most of the team's pitching; they were caught by Morgan Murphy, a Providence native playing his first season in the majors.

King Kelly handled the team well, and demonstrated his knack for fast thinking. The rules of the time allowed substitutions "at any point in the game." During one game, while Kelly was managing from the bench, an opposing batter hit a foul pop-up near the Boston bench which none of the fielders could reach. The Reds' manager simply stood up, announced loudly, "Kelly now catching for Boston!" and caught the ball for an out. (The rule was amended the following year.)

At the end of the season, Boston won the league's first pennant by 6 1/2 games over John Ward's second-place Brooklyn team. Old Hoss Radbourn won 27 games for the Reds in his last great year, and Ad Gumbert had the best year of his career, posting 23 wins. Hardy Richardson led the league in RBIs (although they weren't tabulated in those days) with 146, and Harry Stovey had a league-leading 97 stolen bases.

The rival Beaneaters lagged behind the Reds both in gate receipts and in performance. Few fans went to South End Grounds, as the Boston National Leaguers slumped to a fifth-place finish.

In 1890, it was the gamesmanship off the field that mattered most. The competing leagues inflated their attendance and revenue figures, each attempting to show that it was winning the "war." In truth, all of the teams suffered financially. In the Players' League, only Boston ended the season with a profit. The National League clubs, left with few star attractions, did even worse, drawing half the number of spectators as Players' League teams.

On the front line of battle for the National League was its "War Committee," headed by Al Spalding, who had been a hero in Boston when he pitched for the old National Association Red Stockings, but was now president of the Chicago White Stockings and among the most intransigent of the hard-line owners. One of Spalding's tactics was to try to persuade—usually by offering a large sum of money—Brotherhood players to jump back to the National League. Spalding later admitted that he failed in his attempt to get the player he most wanted: King Kelly. The Boston manager turned down Spalding's $10,000 certified check, telling the Chicago owner, "I can't go back on the boys."

By the end of the 1890 season, attendance was dwindling in all cities for all leagues. Fans were tiring of the war taking place behind the scenes, and wanted the focus of attention to go back on playing baseball. Financial backers of the Players' League were

May 9, 1892: Miss Woodbury Knows How to Pitch

Smith College, in Northampton, Massachusetts, was founded as a college for women in 1871 under an endowment from philanthropist Sophia Smith. By the end of the decade, students were playing baseball on campus. With no athletic field available, matches were played on the lawn in front of Hubbard House. After a couple of years, school authorities put a stop to the games, fearing broken windows.

Play had resumed by 1892 with intramural and interclass matches. On May 9, Smith's freshmen and sophomore nines took to the field behind the president's house in a game that generated wide interest. The *Boston Herald* printed a "Special Dispatch" from Northampton describing the events:

THE SMITH GIRLS PLAY BALL
A Freshman Victory—Miss Woodbury Knows How to Pitch

Rumors of blistered hands, skirts minus trains, and of heated discussions of the merits of alcohol versus alum water for hardening hands have floated around town today. Not since the famous snow fort battle, which obtained unenviable publicity, have the athletes of Smith been in such high feather. For yesterday afternoon the game was called, and Smith played great ball.

The sophomores won the toss, and went to the bat. The freshman battery received the class yell and much waving of the freshman colors (green) as they took position.

The pitcher, Miss Woodbury, clad in black, wore glasses and her hair in a long braid. She, however, pitched a good game. The catcher, Miss Long, daughter of ex-Gov. Long, a decided blonde, looked well, even in the mask and gloves. She held Miss Woodbury's curves in good style.

In the first inning the sophs got in two runs, owing chiefly to the fact that the centre field caught in her dress skirt, and when the umpire said "A muff," the centre field responded: "No, my skirt, Mary."

When the freshmen got after the ball they showed a decidedly improved style of sprinting, and pounded out nine runs, in spite of the efforts of the entire field to get under a ball.

Two, instead of three, put the side out, and in various ways it differed from the regular game. The umpire, a pretty girl in blue, was heard to murmur "I beg your pardon," as she declared the second freshie out.

In the second Miss Woodbury's curves were even more pronounced, and the sophs batted air to a large extent. By the aid of some fumbles and a loss of the ball on the part of the field, they got three runs. The last out died hard, almost on the home plate, owing to a fall over the first baseman's trail.

When the freshies opened the second, it was evident that it was their game,

> *for no sophs could find the terrific drives away out under the apple trees of the campus. Misses Long and Woodbury made four baggers each when the bases were full.*
>
> *The inning was marred by a few mishaps to dresses, whereat the field desisted from regular labor and loaned pins. The sophs' battery, Misses Crehore and Stottart, did not indulge in masks or gloves; and, although Miss Crehore's delivery is amazingly swift, it was not difficult for the freshmen to find the ball for 20 runs.*
>
> *During the third the Misses Long and Woodbury changed places, and Miss Long gave an exhibition of her style of pitching, which, while not so scientific as Miss Woodbury's, was equally effective in keeping her opponents down to three runs.*
>
> *Then the sun being in the umpire's eyes, and dinner hour drawing near, the game adjourned. Score 29 to 9 in favor of the class whose color is green, and whose yell still is "Rah, rah, rah! So-fi-a Smith!"*
>
> The *Herald* account is based on a *Hampshire Gazette* report with the heading "What a Gazette Man Saw from a Roof." Considering his vantage point, the *Gazette's* reporter must have had exceptional ears to be able to hear the conversations that he purported took place on the field.

tiring of losing money on their investment, and were less willing than the established National League owners to ride out the troubled time.

In October, representatives of the Players League gave Al Spalding their unconditional surrender, and the Brotherhood War was over.

ANSONIA BIG GORHAMS

One of the perversities of the color barrier that became established in baseball was that African-Americans born in the United States were barred from organized baseball while Cubans of the same skin color were considered acceptable. As a result, many black clubs included "Cuban" in their team names. One of these was the Cuban Giants, the first all-professional black team, organized in 1885.

The Cuban Giants were an independent club that barnstormed around the country, making their own business arrangements and setting their own schedule. They won 21 of their first 26 games, and were soon recognized as the preeminent African-American team in the nation. When the League of Colored Base Ball Players was formed in 1887, the Cuban Giants declined to join because they were thriving on their own without a league structure. The team was so strong that later, in 1887, the white Eastern League invited the Cuban Giants to become a league franchise, an invitation which the black team turned down.

Starting in 1889, the Cuban Giants did enter organized baseball, but always on their own terms. The team played as a unit, representing various cities, including

Trenton, New Jersey in the Mid-States League and York, Pennsylvania in the Eastern Interstate League.

In 1891, a new Connecticut State League was organized. Two African-American ballplayers had previously broken into the minor leagues with Connecticut teams: Moses Fleetwood Walker with Waterbury in 1885 and 1886, and Frank Grant with Meriden in 1886. The new league included a franchise in Ansonia which was represented by the Cuban Giants under the name "Big Gorhams."

The Ansonia Big Gorhams were among the best teams of any color at any time. Third baseman Sol White was a slugger who never hit less than .333 in a season; during his long career in the game, White was a player, manager, organizer, and historian of early black baseball. Frank Grant, a rifle-armed infielder who had a lifetime batting average of .337 in six minor-league seasons, played second base (in Sol White's 1907 *History of Colored Baseball*, White wrote of his Ansonia teammate: "His playing was a revelation to his fellow teammates, as well as the spectators. In hitting he ranked with the best and his fielding bordered on the impossible.") The Big Gorhams' battery con-

Second baseman Frank Grant is considered by many historians to have been the greatest African-American baseball player of the nineteenth century. Born in Pittsfield, Massachusetts, Grant broke into Organized Baseball in 1886 with Meriden, Connecticut, in the Eastern League. He then played for the Buffalo Bisons in the International League, and so impressed the correspondent for *Sporting Life*, that the writer declared Grant to be the best player Buffalo had ever had—since future Hall-of-Famers Dan Brouthers, Jim Galvin, Jim O'Rourke, and Old Hoss Radbourn had all played for Buffalo, Grant's abilities must have been spectacular. In 1891, Frank Grant was one of the Cuban Giants who represented Ansonia in the Connecticut State League. It was the seventh minor league he played for, and his last season in organized baseball. As baseball's color barrier became more impenetrable, Frank Grant continued to play for black barnstorming teams until retiring after the 1903 "Colored Championship Series." *Photo courtesy of Jerry Malloy.*

View from the upper deck of the South End Grounds' Grand Pavilion, circa 1890. Note the carved columns and the "witches' caps" atop the grandstand roof. This incarnation of the South End Grounds was to be the only double-decked ballpark in Boston history. It lasted less than six years, until fire destroyed the facility in 1894. After the fire, the park had to be rebuilt at a smaller size because it had been underinsured and the team owners couldn't afford to rebuild the second deck. *Photo courtesy of the National Baseball Library & Archive, Cooperstown, N.Y.*

sisted of pitcher George Stovey and catcher Clarence Williams. Stovey, widely regarded as the best African-American pitcher of his time, had already experienced several successful seasons in minor-league baseball, and hard-hitting Williams was one of the most reliable catchers.

The Connecticut State League collapsed before the year was over, however, and the Big Gorhams never again entered the ranks of organized baseball. The team resumed its barnstorming practice, and ended 1891 with a cumulative record of 96 wins and only 4 defeats.

TWO CHAMPIONS

Since its founding in 1882, the American Association enjoyed its greatest success in Midwestern cities such as St. Louis, Louisville, Cincinnati, and Kansas City. The league's policies in favor of Sunday baseball and liquor sales in ballparks were met more favorably in this part of the country than they would have been in the East (Boston, for example, did not allow baseball to be played on Sundays until 1929). For the first nine

The 1892 National League champion Boston Beaneaters. The man in the derby is Frank Selee, an Amherst, New Hampshire native, who managed the club from 1890 to 1901 and led them to 1,000 victories and five pennants. The 1892 team included five future Hall-of-Famers: Kid Nichols, John Clarkson (at far right, in sweater), Hugh Duffy, Tommy McCarthy, and Mike "King" Kelly. Although past his prime, Kelly was still the team's star attraction, as indicated by the bold letttering on his jersey. One of the most colorful and popular stars of the era, Kelly's image appeared on dime novels, tobacco cards, and lithographs (Boston paid him $2,000 to play baseball and $3,000 for "use of his picture"). Kelly toured on stage and songs were written in his honor—a phonograph cylinder of "Slide, Kelly, Slide" was one of the top hits of 1892. Unfortunately, King Kelly devoted himself more to drinking and carousing than to playing baseball, and his lifestyle had taken its toll by the time of this photograph. Kelly batted only .189 in 78 games in 1892, his last season in Boston. He died two years later at age 36. *Photo courtesy of the Boston Public Library, Print Department.*

years of its existence, the American Association fielded no teams in New England. That changed after the Brotherhood War.

The Association had tried to remain a neutral party to the war of 1890. Relations with the National League had never been very positive—the senior circuit derisively referred to the American Association as "The Beer and Whiskey League"—so the junior league refused to take sides in the Brotherhood War and hoped to ride it out. Losses to the American Association teams were at least as severe as those to the Players' and National League clubs, however, and three of the Association's eight teams dropped out before the 1891 season.

For the "rebels" who had thrown their lots with the failed Players' League, the American Association provided an attractive alternative to returning to the hated National League. The Boston Reds team that had won the Players' League championship entered the American Association as a replacement for one of the three teams the Association had lost.

Nearly the entire Reds roster made the jump: King Kelly, Dan Brouthers, Tom Brown, Hardy Richardson, Morgan Murphy, Harry Stovey, and Arthur Irwin. For several of these men, it was the third Boston major-league team they were to play for in three years. King Kelly was immediately loaned out to Cincinnati, however, to help attract fans to that shaky franchise. Harry Stovey, after signing with the Association, broke his contract by then signing with the Beaneaters, joining Billy Nash and Joe Quinn, who had already returned to the Boston National League team.

With Kelly's departure, Arthur Irwin was appointed manager, and important additions were made to the roster. Hugh Duffy was brought to Boston to play right field, and veteran pitcher Charlie Buffinton was signed to join George Haddock and Darby O'Brien in a three-man pitching rotation. Joining Dan Brouthers in the infield were second baseman Cub Stricker, shortstop Paul Revere Radford of Roxbury, and third baseman Duke Farrell, from Oakdale, Massachusetts.

Opening day for the American Association Boston Reds was played on April 18 before a packed crowd at the Congress Street Grounds. The Reds won on a home run by Hugh Duffy, and continued to win as the season progressed. By July 4, they were far out in first place with a 44–22 record, and ended the season as champions, 8 1/2 games ahead of Charles Comiskey's St. Louis Browns. Boston players dominated the American Association offensively: Dan Brouthers led the league in batting (.350) and slugging average; Tom Brown led in hits, runs, triples, and stolen bases (106); Duke Farrell led in home runs and tied Hugh Duffy for the top spot in RBIs. The pitching staff did its part, too: George Haddock had a career-high 34 wins, while Charlie Buffinton garnered 29.

The National League Boston Beaneaters of 1891 relied more on their pitching than their hitting. Iron man John Clarkson won 33 games; Kid Nichols, in his second major-league season won 30, and Harry Staley, acquired after the start of the season, won 20. The rest of the line-up was reliable, though not spectacular. As the Boston Reds cruised to their championship, the Beaneaters were locked in a tight three-way race for the title. Hoping to strengthen the team's offense, manager Frank Selee signed King Kelly again despite the fact that he was already under contract to the American Association. Kelly returned to play sixteen games for the Beaneaters down the home stretch. On the strength of a fourteen-game winning streak in the final weeks of the season, Boston took the National League pennant.

For the first—and only—time in its history, Boston had two major-league champion teams. The idea of a postseason series between the two clubs was raised early, and the Reds did issue a challenge to their National League counterparts. Unfortunately for Hub baseball fans, the Beaneaters refused to play the American Association title holders.

For the second year in a row, a league dominated by the Boston Reds folded after they won the title. Heavy financial losses, and brazen raids on its players by the

May 30, 1894: Crowd Goes Wild Over Lowe's Batting

On May 15, 1894, while a game was in progress with the Baltimore Orioles, Boston's magnificent South End Grounds caught fire and burned to the ground. Until the park could be rebuilt, the Beaneaters played their home games at the Congress Street Grounds, former home of the Players' League and American Association Boston teams. Two weeks after moving into the new accommodations, Boston's 150-pound second baseman Bobby Lowe became the first player in major-league history to hit four home runs in a game. Lowe achieved the feat in the second game of a doubleheader with Cincinnati, all of his homers coming off Reds pitcher Ice Box Chamberlain. Boston had won the first game (Lowe went hitless in six at-bats) 13–10, and aided by Lowe's batting, took the afternoon game 20–11. Although the left field fence in the Congress Street Grounds was only 250 feet from home plate, the *Boston Globe* report the next day stressed that Lowe's clouts would have been good in any ballpark:

CHEERED BOBBY
Crowd Goes Wild Over Lowe's Batting

It was holiday baseball at the Congress st grounds yesterday.

In the morning, before 3000 people, the home team pulled out a victory by making nine runs in the eighth inning.

The afternoon game was witnessed by 8500 people, and they enjoyed some of the finest hitting ever seen in this country.

Bobby Lowe broke all league records with four home runs in succession, and then tied the record for totals by adding a single, making a total of 17 bases.

The hitting of Lowe has never been surpassed in a game. His home runs were on line drives far over the fence, and would be good for four bases on an open prairie.

The crowd cheered Bobby every time he came up, and when he responded with a home run even the visitors had to join in the good-natured smile.

The players looked tired as they left the field, and every one was satisfied with the way the old ball was hammered around during the day. The score [of the second game]:

BOSTON

	AB	R	BH	TB	PO	A	E
Lowe, 2	6	4	5	17	2	2	1
Long, s	3	5	2	6	2	4	2
Duffy, m	5	0	1	1	1	0	0
T.McCarthy, l	6	2	3	4	3	0	0
Nash, 3	4	3	3	3	0	1	0
Tucker, 1	2	1	0	0	10	2	0
Bannon, r	4	2	2	2	1	0	0

CINCINNATI

	AB	R	BH	TB	PO	A	E
Hoy, m	5	1	1	1	3	0	1
J. McCarthy, 1	5	2	2	2	9	0	1
Latham, 3	4	3	2	4	0	3	2
Holliday, l	4	3	2	8	1	1	0
McPhee, 2	5	0	2	2	4	5	0
Vaughn, c	5	1	2	5	3	3	1
Canavan, r	5	1	1	4	2	0	0

Ryan, c	5	2	2	3	5	0	0	*Smith, s*	5	0	1	2	1	5	1
Nichols, p	5	1	1	1	3	2	0	*Chamberlain, p*	5	0	1	2	1	0	0
Totals	40	20	19	37	27	11	3	*Totals*	43	11	14	30	24	17	6

Innings	1	2	3	4	5	6	7	8	9		
Boston	2	0	9	0	1	5	2	1		—	20
Cincinnati	2	0	0	0	4	0	0	0	5	—	11

Earned runs Boston 7, Cincinnati 8. Two-base hits, T. McCarthy, Ryan, Latham 2, Chamberlain, Long, Smith. Home runs, Holliday 2, Lowe 4, Long, Vaughn, Canavan. Stolen bases, Long, Duffy, Nash 2, Hoy, Latham. Sacrifice hits, Duffy. First base on balls, Long 2, Tucker 3, Nash 2, Hannan, Latham. Struck out, Hannon, Ryan, T. McCarthy, Vaughn, McPhee, Chamberlain. Passed ball, Vaughn. Wild pitches, Nichols, Chamberlain. Hit by pitched ball, Long, Tucker. Umpire, Swartswood. Time 2 h 10 m. Attendance 3500.

— T.H. Murnane.

Box score note: "m" denotes center field.

The "T. H. Murnane" who reported the game was the same Tim Murnane who had played first base for the original Boston Red Caps in 1876.

Bobby Lowe ended the 1894 season with a career-high 17 home runs (second in the league to Hugh Duffy's 18). Lowe played another thirteen years in the major-leagues, but never again hit more than seven homers in a season.

National League—such as the one that brought King Kelly back to the Beaneaters—doomed the American Association. In December of 1891, the Association collapsed, with four of its stronger clubs being annexed by the National League. The Boston Reds ceased to exist after winning championships in both of its two years as a major-league ball club.

For the Boston Beaneaters, their 1891 title was to be the first of three consecutive National League pennants.

Thirty-year-old Frank Selee made his major-league managerial debut in 1890, when he was given the difficult task of assembling a Beaneaters roster to replace the one that had jumped to the Players' League. He ended up remaining at the helm for a dozen years, leading the team to five National League championships. Selee was considered a "player's manager" nearly a century before it became fashionable; his stated philosophy was, "If I make things pleasant for the players, they reciprocate."

Through the turmoil of the Brotherhood War and the competition from the Boston Reds, Selee put together the nucleus of a team that was to be one of the most successful in Boston history. His first important acquisition was Charles "Kid" Nichols, who made his big-league debut on April 23, 1890, and remained with the team throughout Selee's tenure with the club, winning 329 games during those twelve seasons. Bobby Lowe, originally an outfielder who was later moved to second base, also entered the majors in 1890 and also went on to play every year that Selee managed the team. Tommy Tucker, from Holyoke, Massachusetts, was another player whom Selee picked up for his first team; Tucker, a slick-fielding, hot-tempered first baseman who enjoyed fisticuffs as much as he did baseball, held down the position until 1897. Shortstop Herman "The Flying Dutchman" Long also joined the Beaneaters in 1890, and remained with the team through 1902.

The return of Billy Nash and Joe Quinn, and the addition of Harry Stovey, helped the Beaneaters win the 1891 pennant. The collapse of the American Association prior to the 1892 season made additional players available to strengthen the club for that season. Two of these additions were Hugh Duffy from the Boston Reds, and Tommy McCarthy, who had played for the Boston Unions in 1884 and the Beaneaters in 1885; together, outfielders Duffy and McCarthy became known as the "Heavenly Twins." Another former Association player who came to Boston in 1892 was pitcher Happy Jack Stivetts, who had won 33 games for the St. Louis Browns in 1891 and led the league in strikeouts with 259.

With the National League having expanded to twelve teams in 1892, league officials decided to play a split season, with the winner of the first half of the season to play the winner of the second half in a post-season series to determine the championship. Led by the pitching of Kid Nichols and Jack Stivetts, each of whom won 35 games, Boston won the first half with a record of 52–22, and came in second to the Cleveland Spiders in the latter half of the season. Although the Beaneaters had a cumulative season record 8 1/2 games better than Cleveland, the two teams met in a best-of-nine series for the pennant.

The first game of the championship series was played in Cleveland on October 17, with the Spiders' Cy Young matched against Jack Stivetts. Both pitchers went the distance in an 11-inning scoreless tie, until the game was called because of darkness. That was as close as Cleveland would come to winning a game in the series. Boston swept the next five games to take the championship.

Having established a winning lineup, the Beaneaters made few changes to it in 1893. Bobby Lowe was shifted to second base to replace Joe Quinn, and veteran Cliff Carroll joined the club to take the outfield spot where Lowe had been. The split-season concept was abandoned, and after Boston won its third straight pennant, there was no post-season series to cap off the year.

In 1894, the Beaneaters lost their home of the previous six years. During a game on May 15, boys set fire to some rubbish under the right field stands of South End Grounds, and the magnificent ballpark burned down (while it burned, Boston's Tommy Tucker and Baltimore's John McGraw happily continued the fist-fight they had been engaged in near third base). The flames spread throughout the neighborhood, destroying almost two hundred buildings in a 12-acre area, including a school and an engine house. There were no reported deaths, but one thousand families were left homeless.

The Beaneaters played their remaining home games at the hitter-friendly Congress Street Grounds. Highlights of the 1894 season included Bobby Lowe's four-homer game on May 30, and Hugh Duffy's performance over the course of the entire year:

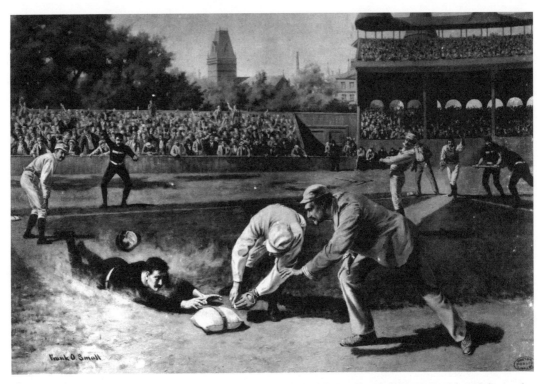

Prints of this painting by Frank O. Small entitled "Slide, Kelly, Slide" were sold widely in the 1890s. It was one of many merchandising ventures that profited from King Kelly's popularity. This scene is set in the South End Grounds. It is unclear how the catcher managed to throw the ball, since he has his mitt on one hand and is holding his mask with the other. *Photo courtesy of the Boston Public Library, Print Department.*

These circa 1895 promotional cards came in packages of Mayo Cut Plug Tobacco. The images shown here are of the Beaneaters' Hugh Duffy (left) and Tommy McCarthy (right). Duffy and McCarthy played next to each other in the Boston outfield from 1892 to 1895. Their deft fielding won them the nickname the "Heavenly Twins." Both were later voted into the Hall of Fame (although the reason for McCarthy's election is one of baseball's enduring mysteries). *Photos courtesy of Transcendental Graphics.*

Sep. 16, 1895: A Red Letter Day for Springfield's Baseball Cranks

In 1884, the same year that Providence won major-league baseball's first World's Championship, the Eastern League began operations, soon developing into one of the strongest minor leagues in the country. After the Providence Grays ceased to be a National League franchise, they entered the Eastern League and won its pennant in 1894. The next year, the Ponies of Springfield, Massachusetts, fought the Grays for first place all season and captured the title. The entire city—especially the "cranks," as fans were then called—celebrated Springfield's first baseball championship. The Ponies then faced Providence in a post-season series for the Steinert Cup. The annual battle for this trophy was played between the new league champions and the title holders of the previous season. The Springfield *Union* gave front-page coverage to the outcome of the series opener:

THE FIRST BLOOD
Ponies Won the Opening Game of the Cup Series
A GREAT RECEPTION
New Champions Welcomed Home by 3000 Cranks
BAND PLAYED AND FLAGS WAVED

It was a red letter day for Springfield's baseball cranks and one that will not be forgotten in many a long year.

The home coming of Springfield's first championship baseball team, the celebration in honor of that event, the music, parades, speechmaking, cheers upon cheers and, to crown it all, the opening of the long anticipated Steinert cup series between the two bitterest rivals in the pennant race, the champions and the ex-champions, with a victory for the home team before one of the biggest crowds that ever witnessed a baseball game in this city.

Pandemonium reigned for a time. It marked the climax of the greatest baseball season Springfield has ever known and was the only possible result of the fever of enthusiasm that the Ponies have worked up by their grand race all season, setting the pace all the way from the first and spurting down the stretch for a lead of four or five lengths at the wire.

Even fans from Holyoke—Springfield's traditional rival—cheered the Ponies, according to the *Union*:

The cranks stood on their feet and yelled. The quieter sort applauded with hands and feet, even the big Holyoke delegation joined in to swell the volume of applause, forgetting for the time being their real feelings in their admiration for the new champions and in the resistless [sic] spirit of the occasion, and later through-

out the game it was noticed that Holyoke's applause was equally divided whenever fast or brilliant plays by either team called for it, until both cranks and players were ready to swear by Holyoke for so magnanimously forgiving Springfield for winning the championship.

The game itself was a triumph from a Springfield standpoint: the Ponies outscored the Grays 8–3, highlighted by an inside-the-park home run off the bat of centerfielder Jones. The style of Providence's play—especially that of third baseman Charley Bassett—did not meet with the *Union's* approval:

The contest was one of those clean games in which Springfield crankdom delights with hardly a suspicion of trickery or objectional [sic] tactics. Charley Bassett did get in Jones' way as he rounded third base on his home run drive, compelling Jones to push him out of the way, and lose much time in going it that he was nearly caught at the plate. Thereafter Bassett was greeted with hisses and every time he came to the plate and the crowd exhibited such an ugly feeling in general that he desisted from his usual work during the rest of the game. It may be baseball from Bassett's and Providence's standpoint to block every runner at third so as to make them lose several seconds in touching that bag or to throw them out of step so as to get caught at the plate, but it is not baseball from a Springfield standpoint. The Ponies have always played the cleanest of clean baseball unless compelled to adopt disagreeable tactics by the visitors in retaliation, content to win or lose a game on its honest, open merits, and they have educated Springfield cranks up to the appreciation of a game of that sort.

The score:

SPRINGFIELD

	AB	R	B	PO	A	E
Shannon, s.s.	5	1	2	3	2	3
Leahey, l.f.	5	1	2	2	0	1
Jones, c.f.	4	1	1	3	0	0
Lynch, 3b	4	1	1	1	3	0
Scheffler, r.f.	5	1	0	0	0	0
Glibert, 1b	4	1	1	12	0	0
Gunson, cr	4	0	3	5	0	1
McDonald, 2b	3	1	1	1	4	0
Coughlin, p	3	1	0	0	2	0
Totals	37	8	11	27	11	5

PROVIDENCE

	AB	R	B	PO	A	E
Lyons, c.f.	5	0	0	1	0	0
Bassett, 3b	5	0	1	1	2	0
Knight, l.f.	5	1	3	4	0	1
Rogers, 1b	4	1	1	11	0	0
Cooney, s.s.	4	1	1	3	2	1
Stricker, 2b	4	0	1	1	3	0
Murray, r.f.	4	0	0	2	0	0
Dixon, c	3	0	1	3	1	2
Rudderham, p	4	0	0	1	1	0
Totals	38	3	8	27	9	4

Innings	1	2	3	4	5	6	7	8	9		
Springfield	2	0	9	0	1	5	2	1		—	20
Providence	2	0	0	0	4	0	0	0	5	—	11

Earned runs, Providence 2; total bases, Springfield 17, Providence, 11; stolen bases, Shannon, Lynch, Scheffler, McDonald, Coughlin, Cooney, Stricker 2, Dixon; two-base hits, Leahey,

Gunson 2, Knight 2, Rogers; home run, Jones; first base on balls, Jones, McDonald, Coughlin, Rogers, Cooney, Dixon; first base on errors, Springfield 2, Providence 2; left on bases, Springfield 6, Providence 11; struck out, McDonald, Murray, Rudderham 2; batter hit, Lynch; time 1.50; umpire, Gaffney.

Springfield won three of the next five games in the series to capture the Steinert Cup. It was to be the Ponies' only championship. Providence regained the title in 1896.

Duffy set the all-time record for a single season batting average with a .440 mark, and also topped the league in home runs and RBIs to take the hitting Triple Crown (an accomplishment not yet acknowledged in 1894).

Despite Boston's strong offensive performance, and solid pitching by Kid Nichols and Jack Stivetts, the team ended the season in a disappointing third-place. That was to be its highest finish during a three-year slump.

MINOR SUCCESSES

Dozens of minor leagues had formed during the 1880s, with most of them surviving only a year or less. In the 1890s, several well-organized minor league circuits were established that continued to operate for decades, fielding talented teams and earning strong support from local communities. One of these was the Eastern League, which reorganized in 1892, and at various times included Hartford, Providence, Springfield, and Worcester among its members (renamed the International League in 1912, it continues to this day).

The New England League, after its tentative start in the 1880s, resumed operation in 1891, with teams in Lowell, Lynn, Manchester, Portland, Salem, and Worcester. Lewiston, Maine, and Woonsocket, Rhode Island, joined a month into the season. The league was still shaky; Lowell, Lynn, and Salem failed to finish the season, and only two franchises were financially stable at the close of the first year: Woonsocket and the pennant-winning Portland club. The league regrouped the following year, again fielding eight teams. Again, only five finished, with Woonsocket winning the championship. By the mid-1890s, the New England League had stabilized and its franchises had become stronger. The most successful was Fall River, which won four consecutive titles from 1893 through 1896.

These minor leagues served as a training ground for up-and-coming ballplayers, much as they do today. Napoleon Lajoie, with Fall River in 1896, and Christy Mathewson were two of the baseball all-time greats who got their starts in organized baseball with the New England League of the 1890s. Christy Mathewson made his professional debut on July 21, 1899 as the starting pitcher for Taunton, Massachusetts, against Manchester, New Hampshire. Mathewson lost that game and posted a dismal season record of 2–13, but it was while with Taunton that he continued to develop the "fadeaway" (screwball) pitch that he'd learned the year before. Mathewson went on to win 373 games in the major leagues, and was one of the five charter members elected to the Baseball Hall of Fame. The Taunton ballfield where Mathewson pitched is still in use today, and a commemorative plaque notes the fact that the celebrated pitcher once played there.

The minors were also used by big-league clubs to give a player a little additional seasoning. In 1894, Brown University star Fred Tenney made the jump from college to the National League Boston Beaneaters. When the young catcher initially proved to be something of a disappointment, Boston sent him down to get some professional experience. Tenney played parts of 1895 and 1896 with New Bedford of the New England League and Springfield of the Eastern League before returning to Boston. He went on to enjoy a 17-year career in the major leagues, playing in almost two thousand games.

The New England League also launched the career of a future Hall of Fame umpire. Tommy Connolly of Natick, Massachusetts was born in England and never played baseball, but began umpiring games for a YMCA League in Natick. He came to the attention of New England League president Tim Hurst (himself a former National League umpire) and began umpiring professionally in 1894. After four years, he moved up to the National League, but quit when league officials refused to back him up in a dispute with a player. Connolly then umpired the first game in American League history, in 1901, and remained with the AL for more than half a century, serving as an active umpire for 31 years and the league's umpire-in-chief for another twenty-three.

In the nineteenth century, there were no retirement plans for ballplayers. Most went back down the professional ranks, continuing to play in the minor leagues after their big-leagues careers were over. Jerry Denny, who had played third base for the National League Providence Grays from 1881 through 1885, played professional ball for 25 years; his final six seasons were in the Connecticut State League, with Derby, Waterbury, Norwich, and Bridgeport. First baseman Tommy Tucker, who began his career with Springfield in the 1884 Connecticut State League and went on to star with the Boston Beaneaters in the 1890s, also ended his career back in Connecticut, with New London and Meriden. Left-handed pitcher Matt Kilroy set the all-time major-league strike out record when he fanned 513 batters in his rookie season of 1886, and pitched for Boston in the Players' League four years later; he hurled his final professional game in the last year of the nineteenth century, for Hartford in the Eastern League. Also closing his professional career in the Eastern League was infielder Tom Burns, a veteran of 13 seasons in the majors; Burns played second base for Springfield in 1893 and 1894, while also serving as the team's manager; the next year, solely in a managerial role, he led Springfield to the league championship. One of the former stars who played under Burns was slugger Big Dan Brouthers, who had won five major-league batting titles in eighteen seasons; with Springfield in 1897, Brouthers hit .415 to take the Eastern League hitting title.

Most minor-leaguers never reached the majors, and of those who did make it, most didn't remain in the big leagues long. For these players, minor league baseball was their livelihood, a way to earn a salary for playing baseball. An example of such a

Right: The Steinert Cup awarded to the Springfield, Massachusetts Ponies, winners of the 1895 Eastern League championship. The title was the first ever won by a Springfield team in any league.

Below: One of the brightest stars ever to burst on the baseball scene was Louis "Chief" Sockalexis, a Penobscot Indian from Old Town, Maine. Sockalexis is shown here (back row, second from left) with the 1895 team of Holy Cross College in Worcester, Massachusetts. In April of 1897, he made his major-league debut as an outfielder with the National League Cleveland Spiders. An all-around athlete with enormous natural talent, Sockalexis was immediately acknowledged to be a faster runner and have a stronger throwing arm than any other player in the game. He was also a superb slugger, and batted .338 in his first year. Sadly, Sockalexis started drinking heavily during his rookie season, and was to play only 28 more games in the major leagues. He returned to New England, where he played a couple of more years in the minors, before alcoholism completely debilitated him. The memory of his brief flash of glory remained strong in the minds of Cleveland fans, however; a year after Sockalexis' early death, they voted to name the Cleveland American League club the "Indians" in his honor. *Photo courtesy of the Holy Cross Archives.*

Ponies Won Out Handsomely in Providence Yesterday.

Aug. 1, 1896: A Slugging Bee in Pawtucket

One of the greatest players in baseball history was Napoleon Lajoie, from Woonsocket, Rhode Island. Lajoie began his career at age nineteen, playing semi-pro ball for the home town team while working as a sweeper in a textile mill. In 1896, he made the jump to the New England League, playing center field for Fall River. On July 2 of that year, he went six-for-seven in a game against Pawtucket and led Fall River to a 31–5 drubbing of the Rhode Island club. One month later, Pawtucket got revenge against first-place Fall River, as described in the *Providence Journal*:

A SLUGGING BEE
The Great and Only Phenoms Have Acquired a New Title
Will Be Known Hereafter as the Leather Sluggers
They Pounded Out 32 Runs in Yesterday's Game with Fall River
Pawtucket 32, Fall River 12

Pawtucket Lodge, No. 1, Independent Order of Leather Sluggers, held a three-hour's session on the Dexter street grounds. There was no secretness about the business transacted and the docket was a lengthy one. Manager Smith's men had the Fall River players in the air most of the time and when they fell the thud must have been perceptible in the Border City. The Pawtuckets batted three pitchers out of the box and were beginning to flirt with Hi Ladd's benders when the game was brought to a close. A total of 62 bases was the extent of the business done by the Pawtucket sluggers during their nine innings of swiping, which establishes a new record in batting for professional ball playing. The horse hide was sent in every old direction, first over against the right field fence, over in the yard of the Fales & Jenks Company, up against the dwellings out on Dexter street and to the chicken coop in centre field.

Everything went, especially the balls that collided with the bats in the hands of the Pawtucket players. It was biff, bang from the start, and the Pawtucket players fatted up their batting averages in great shape. There never appeared to be more than one man out, and runs were pushed over the rubber in a manner which brought much pleasure to the 2000 spectators in attendance.

Sandwiched in at occasional intervals there were some neat plays, but batting was the feature.

The score:

PAWTUCKET	ab	r	1b	po	a	e	FALL RIVER	ab	r	1b	po	a	e
Smith, r. f.	7	4	4	1	0	0	McDermott, 2b	6	2	3	0	3	2
Hannivan, s. s.	8	3	6	1	2	0	Rupert, c	6	1	1	9	0	1
Waldron, l. f.	7	5	4	2	0	0	Ladd, l. f., p	6	2	2	3	0	1

Yeager, c	7	5	4	6	1	0	Lajoie, c. f., 3b, l. f.	5	2	3	1	0	1
Whiting, c. f.	7	5	4	1	1	1	Geier, r. f., c. f.	5	2	4	2	1	0
Beaumont, 1b	7	4	5	9	1	0	Kennedy, 1b	5	1	1	6	0	0
News, 2b	8	2	3	3	6	0	Reilley, s. s.	5	1	2	2	1	0
Coughlin, 3b	7	3	5	3	0	2	Lyons, 3b, p	4	1	3	4	0	0
Lincoln, p	7	1	0	1	3	0	Klobedanz, p	2	0	0	0	1	0
Totals	65	32	35	27	14	3	Dunn, p, r. f.	3	0	0	0	0	0
							Totals	47	12	19	27	6	5

Innings	1	2	3	4	5	6	7	8	9		
Pawtucket	3	0	6	2	4	8	8	0	1	—	32
Fall River	0	4	2	1	0	4	1	0	0	—	12

Earned runs—Pawtucket 18; Fall River 7. *Two-base hits*—Smith 2, Hannivan 2, Waldron 2, Yeager 2, Whiting 3, Beaumont, Coughlin 2, McDermott, Ladd, Lajoie, Geier. *Three-base hits*—Hannivan, Beaumont. *Home runs*—Smith, Beaumont, Coughlin, Lyons. *First base on balls*—By Lincoln—Lajoie, Geier; by Klobedanz—Whiting; by Dunn—Waldron, Lincoln; by Lyons—Yeager, Smith. *First base on errors*—Pawtucket 5; Fall River 2. *Struck out*—By Lincoln—Rupert, Ladd, Reilley, Klobedanz, Dunn; by Klobedanz—Hannivan, Waldron, Yeager, Coughlin, Lincoln 2; by Lyons—News. *Passed balls*—Rupert 2. *Wild pitches*—Lyons 3, Lincoln. *Hit by pitched ball*—By Dunn—Coughlin; by Lincoln—Kennedy. *Umpires*—Connolly, Dunn, Horner and Klobedanz. *Time*—3 hours.

(Box score note: Dunn and Klobedanz helped umpire when they weren't playing.)

Nap Lajoie played only six more games in the New England League. He was leading the league in batting with a .429 average when he was signed by Philadelphia in the National League. Lajoie made his major-league debut on August 12, and played thirty-nine games, batting .326, for Philadelphia through the rest of the 1896 season. He went on to play 21 years in the major leagues, and was one of the first players elected to the Baseball Hall of Fame.

ballplayer is Fred "Duke" Klobedanz, a left-handed pitcher from Waterbury, Connecticut. Klobedanz won a total of 287 wins in seventeen professional seasons—53 of his victories came in the major leagues and 234 in the minors. His entire career was spent with New England teams, including two full seasons with the Boston Beaneaters in 1897 and 1898. He also pitched for Worcester in the Eastern League, and for New England League teams in Portland, Lewiston, Dover, Fall River, Lawrence, New Bedford, and Brockton. In the winters, he worked as a carpenter, doing repairs on the ballparks in which he played.

Although the larger minor leagues became more firmly established in the 1890s, smaller state leagues still had a difficult time surviving (and always would). The Rhode

Island League that had begun in 1889 folded after the 1891 season. Several Connecticut leagues started and disbanded until a sustainable one was organized in 1897. A Maine State League launched in 1897 lasted only two seasons. In 1899, there were fewer minor leagues than had existed ten years earlier, but they were far more stable, and many of them would continue for decades.

BEANEATERS BACK ON TOP

After winning three National League pennants from 1891 through 1893, the Boston Beaneaters watched from a vantage point no higher than third place as their main rivals of the decade, the Baltimore Orioles, won the title in each of the next three seasons. Managed by Ned Hanlon, the Orioles were a rowdy, brawling team that included such scrappers as John McGraw, Wee Willie Keeler, and Hughie Jennings. Throughout the decade, meetings between the Beaneaters and the Orioles often resembled gang fights more than baseball games. It was particularly satisfying for the Beaneaters and their supporters therefore when the Boston club went into Baltimore in the closing days of the 1897 season and defeated Hanlon's gang to win the pennant.

Boston repeated as champions in 1898, and again Baltimore was the team that finished just behind them in the standings.

Manager Frank Selee's starting line-up remained intact through the final three years of the decade. Hugh Duffy was still in the outfield, where he had been joined by Chick Stahl, who hit .354 in his rookie season of 1897, and "Sliding Billy" Hamilton, who three times stole more than 100 bases in a season. Bobby Lowe and Herman Long remained the team's keystone combination. At first base, Brown University alumnus Fred Tenney had replaced Tommy Tucker. Billy Nash was gone after ten years with the team; taking over his position was Jimmy Collins, who proved to be one of the best fielding third basemen of all time. Boston's catcher from 1896 through 1899 was Marty Bergen from North Brookfield, Massachusetts, whom Selee described as "not in his right mind"; the disturbed catcher proved his manager correct after the 1899 season, when he murdered his family with an axe and then killed himself.

Kid Nichols continued to reign as Boston's—and the league's—best pitcher, leading the National League in wins three straight years from 1896 through 1898. Fred Klobedanz, up from Fall River for his first full season with Boston in 1897, was close behind Nichols, with a 26–7 record that led the league in winning percentage. Welsh-born Ted "Parson" Lewis, who had pitched for Williams College, also played his first full season in 1897, and contributed 21 victories. Lewis, an ordained minister, got his master's degree from Williams and quit baseball before he was thirty years old to become an educator; he later served as president of the University of Massachusetts, and then of the University of New Hampshire.

In 1898, Boston manager Frank Selee introduced baseball's first four-man pitching rotation. Three of them were 20-game winners: Kid Nichols, with a league-leading 31; Ted Lewis, with 26; and Vic Willis, who notched 25 wins as a rookie. Fred Klobedanz won a respectable 19 games as the team's fourth starter, but he was to win only two more games in the majors before being sent down to the minors for the remainder for his career.

The 1897 varsity baseball team of Bowdoin College in Brunswick, Maine. Bowdoin was among the first colleges in the country to take up baseball. Its senior class team played the Sunrise Club of Brunswick in 1860, and a 1864 match with visiting Harvard did much to popularize the game in Maine. Bowdoin reigned as champions of the state from 1865 through 1867. In 1885, four Maine colleges—Bates, Bowdoin, Colby, and University of Maine—played the first of what became an annual tournament to determine a state college champion. Bowdoin won that first championship in 1885, and the team pictured here tied for the 1897 title with University of Maine. *Photo courtesy of the Bowdoin College Special Collections Library.*

Game action in Baltimore's Oriole Park on September 27, 1897. The Beaneaters pounded four Orioles pitchers in this game for a 19–10 win that clinched the National League championship for Boston (the *Boston Herald*'s front-page report of the contest was headlined "Baltimore Was Annihilated"). The game was played before 30,000 Baltimore partisans; an even greater achivement for the Hub team than their victory was that they managed to get out of the city alive afterward.

Oct. 4, 1897: Moonlight and Mosquitoes

The National League expanded from eight teams to twelve in 1892, adding several clubs from the defunct American Association. With only one major league, and many teams far out of the pennant race toward the end of the season, league owners sought a way to stimulate public interest. In 1894, the Temple Cup was introduced: a post-season series between the first and second place teams would be played, with the winner to be given a silver trophy donated by wealthy Pittsburgh sportsman William Temple. For the first three years of the series, Boston failed to finish as one of the league's top two clubs. In 1897, the Beaneaters won the pennant by two games over the Baltimore Orioles, and on October 4 played their first game for the Temple Cup at South End Grounds. Although conditions were far from optimal, Boston eked out a win. As reported in the *Boston Post* the following day:

FIRST TEMPLE CUP GAME PLAYED IN THE DARK.
ONE LAP IN THE RACE FOR VICTORY.
First Game in the Temple Cup Series Won by Boston.
THE SCORE WAS 13 TO 12.
Darkness Almost Spoiled the Home Team's Chances,
but They Pulled Out Unharmed.

The moon was high, the stars were out, the hush of evening had come down; the sky was all brown and gray with the farewell of sunset, and around the darkened field 10,000 people strove to distinguish the Bostons and the Baltimores in the gloom.

And then they heard a hollow crack as Kelley struck at the ball. They saw Long on the third base line as if bewildered, dodging right and left. They saw his arms thrown awkwardly outward as if groping blindly for something he knew was coming but could not see; they saw him stumble and make the motion of throwing; they saw Tenney at first clap his hands together and toss something on the ground; they heard the umpire shout and wave his arms. Then the Baltimore men stopped running bases and rushed toward the gate, and the first game for the Temple cup was won.

It was a moment worthy of rejoicing. Scarcely a man was so brave as to hope that they who were great enough even to win the pennant were fit to prevail against the powers of darkness.

But the good fates were with Boston, and the nightmare of defeat was banished by the lightning of victory.

The game was such a one as would displease the scientists, but it had in it all the elements that appeal to the ordinary observer. There were plenty of misplays and actual errors, and the hero, Nichols, was batted out of the box, but the balance of victory alternated between Boston and Baltimore so often that the lack of science was overlooked.

The visitors were in the lead till the sixth inning, when Boston went to the front with five runs, only to fall back again in the seventh, when Baltimore added two runs to its score.

But in the eighth Boston harvested two, and though darkness favored the visitors in the ninth they failed to regain the lead, although they had men on third and second.

By this time the sun had set, and it was so dark that the ball could hardly be seen. Boston wanted the game postponed, but [umpire] Hurst said, "Play it out!" and they started in by moonlight. The gnats were so thick in the field that players and umpires kept waving their hands to clear the atmosphere, while the cranks yelled, "Call the game!"

Lewis swept aside a few mosquitoes and sent in three balls that Nops could not find. Bergen refused to come up till the second strike had been called, owing to the danger of playing in the dark. McGraw sent one up into the night, but Duffy's sharp eyes soon located it, and McGraw was out. Keeler hit to centre for a base. Jennings hit one somewhere over first base and went to second and Keeler to third while the ball was being found. Kelley hit to Long and was out on a decision which was practically a gift to Boston. Otherwise, they might have been playing all night. The score:

BOSTON

	AB.	R.	B.	TB.	PO.	A.	E.
Hamilton, c.f.	3	2	2	2	3	0	0
Tenney, 1b	2	3	0	0	8	1	1
Lowe, 2b	5	2	2	3	1	4	0
Stahl, r.f.	3	3	1	1	1	0	2
Duffy, l.f.	5	2	3	3	3	0	0
Collins, 3b	5	0	1	1	3	1	1
Long, s.s.	4	1	3	3	2	3	0
Bergen, c	5	0	2	2	5	0	0
Nichols, p	3	0	0	0	1	1	0
Lewis, p	2	0	0	0	0	0	0
Totals	37	13	13	15	27	10	4

BALTIMORE

	AB.	R.	B.	TB.	PO.	A.	E.
McGraw, 3b	6	3	3	3	0	1	1
Keeler, r.f.	6	2	2	2	0	0	0
Jennings, s.s.	6	2	5	7	2	6	0
Kelley, l.f.	6	4	3	5	4	0	0
Stenzel, c.f.	5	1	1	2	1	0	0
Doyle, 1b	5	0	3	3	11	0	1
Reitz, 2b	5	0	1	2	3	2	1
Clarke, c	5	0	1	1	3	1	0
Nops, p	5	0	1	1	0	1	0
Totals	49	12	20	26	24	11	3

Innings	1	2	3	4	5	6	7	8	9		
Boston	3	0	0	1	2	5	0	2		—	13
Baltimore	4	0	1	0	2	3	2	0	0	—	12

Earned runs—Boston, 4; Baltimore, 10. Two-base hits—Lowe, Long, Jennings (2), Kelley (2), Stenzel, Reitz. Sacrifice hit—Tenney. Stolen bases—Hamilton, Stahl, Bergen. First base on balls—By Nops, Hamilton (2), Tenney (2), Stahl (2), Long. First base on errors—Boston, 2; Baltimore, 1. Struck out—by Nichols, Nops (3); by Lewis, Nops; by Nops, Long, Bergen.

> *Wild pitches—Nichols, 1; Nops, 1. Time—2h, 10m. Umpires—Hurst and Emslie. Attendance—11,000.*
>
> This was to be Boston's only victory ever in a Temple Cup game. Baltimore won the next four matches to take the 1897 series, and the trophy was withdrawn before the start of the 1898 season.

Kid Nichols, Vic Willis, and Ted Lewis remained Boston's top pitchers in 1899, but couldn't lead the club to a third pennant, which was won by Brooklyn. For the first time in eight years, the National League championship was not captured by a Boston or Baltimore team. Many baseball fans, tired of the rowdy kind of baseball that had dominated major league play during the decade, openly cheered the fact that the two teams that exemplified rough-and-tumble baseball had failed to be rewarded for it.

Backlash against violence on the ballfield had been brewing for sometime. Venerable Henry Chadwick, who had been writing about baseball since the 1850s, was editor of *Spalding's Baseball Guide* when he wrote in the 1895 edition: "There was but one drawback to the creditable success of the entire championship campaigns of 1894, and that was the unwonted degree of 'hoodlumism' which disgraced the season . . . brutal assaults on umpire and players . . . spiking or wilfully colliding with a base runner, bellowing like a wild bull at the pitcher . . . Managers and captains were alike guilty . . . Is it any wonder that the season of 1894 stands on record as being marked by more disgraceful kicking, rowdy play, blackguard language and brutal play than that of any season since the League was organized?"

Another problem threatening the integrity of the game was 'syndicatism' (called "Freedmanism" by Al Spalding in reference to New York Giants owner Andrew Freedman who was its most outspoken advocate). Some National League owners weren't satisfied with a monopoly on major league baseball. They wanted to form a trust similar to those of the oil and steel industries (such trusts were later outlawed by federal legislation). Freedman and others wanted to turn The National League of Professional Base Ball Clubs into "The National League Base Ball Trust" with each club to be issued a percentage of stock in the syndicate. Clubs would no longer operate independently under this scheme; they would all be shareholders of one big business.

By the late 1890s, baseball fans were demanding cleaner baseball from the players and greater integrity from the owners.

In the 1880's, the National League openly ridiculed the "loose morals" of American Association clubs. Once the senior circuit had a monopoly, however, the game became so violent and corrupt that reform was essential. A new major league was about to be formed; it would attempt to remedy some of the game's problems and would provide the National League with its greatest challenge.

As for the Beaneaters, the dynasty was over. It would be fifteen years until Boston won another National League pennant.

The success of the Boston Beaneaters in the 1890s was due in large part to the pitching of Kid Nichols, shown here in a tobacco card portrait (left) and demonstrating an underhand pitching motion (below). His career with the Boston National Leaguers lasted from 1890 through 1901, a period during which he won 329 games (appropriately, the "Kid" was the youngest pitcher in history to garner 300 wins, reaching that mark before his thirty-first birthday). In an eight-year stretch from 1891 through 1898, Nichols won 30 games or more in seven of those seasons, and led the Beaneaters to five pennants. Nichols pitched without a wind-ups and without a curveball, instead relying on change-ups to keep the batters off-stride. *Photos courtesy of Transcendental Graphics (left) and the Boston Public Library, Print Department (below).*

The Boston Beaneaters' infield of the late 1890's, perhaps the finest infield combination of the 19th century; third baseman Jimmy Collins (on floor), second baseman Bobby Lowe (left), first baseman Fred Tenney (standing), shortstop Herman "Germany" Long (right). Collins, the first third baseman to be enshrined in the Baseball Hall of Fame, revolutionized his position, diving for hard smashes and dashing in to field bunts barehanded. Lead-off batter Bobby Lowe played for Boston from 1890 to 1901, helping lead the team to five National League pennants. Shortstop Herman Long, whose base running skills earned him the nickname "The Flying Dutchman," was the sole defensive weak spot—in 13 seasons with the team, he averaged 70 errors a year, with a league-leading high of 102 in 1892. Fred Tenney, from Georgetown, Massachusetts, had been a left-handed catcher with Brown University. After failing in the majors as both a catcher and an outfielder, Tenney was moved to first base in 1894; he played his new position with unprecedented mobility, and became one of the best defensive first baseman in the history of the game. *Photo courtesy of the Boston Public Library, Print Department.*

Within a few years, the roster that had won the 1898 championship broke up. Billy Hamilton retired; Marty Bergen was dead; Fred Klobedanz was back in the minors. And three players—Jimmy Collins, Chick Stahl, and Ted Lewis—left the Beaneaters to join the Boston franchise in the new American League.

5

1900–1909:
A New Era

With the monopolistic National League unwilling or unable to fix the game's growing problems, there was an opportunity for a new league to take a shot at rehabilitating professional baseball.

Ban Johnson, who had been president of the thriving Western League since 1894, long had the ambition to turn it into a major league. He began to make his move after the 1899 season, when the National League dropped four of its franchises. Johnson renamed his circuit the American League, picked up many of the players who had been cut loose by the Nationals, and put a rival team in Chicago under the management of his chief ally, Charles Comiskey.

Still technically a minor league in 1900, the American League prospered under Johnson's strong leadership. To combat the on-field violence and dirty play that had permeated baseball in the 1890s, Ban Johnson hired top-notch umpires, paid them well, and gave them full authority to maintain discipline on the field. Fans flocked to AL ballparks to see "clean" baseball, and the Sporting News—the most influential baseball publication—noted that the American League was without "the cowardly truckling, alien ownership, syndicatism, hyppodroming [throwing games], selfish jealousies, arrogance of club owners, mercenary spirit, and disregard of public demands" that were so common in the National League.

In the fall of 1900, the American League made plans to invade the East by establishing clubs in Baltimore, Buffalo, Philadelphia, and Washington. Ban Johnson announced that commencing with the 1901 season the American League would operate as a major league on par with the National League. This proclamation triggered open warfare between the two leagues, as they competed for players, cities, fans, and financing.

National League owners, still embroiled in the controversy over forming a baseball trust (an issue that wouldn't be settled until December, 1901, when they voted against such a syndicate) were factionalized, and unable to present a united front (they were unable even to elect a league president).

The senior circuit was dealt a one-two punch by Ban Johnson when former NL stalwarts Connie Mack and John McGraw were given partial ownership to establish American League teams in Philadelphia and Baltimore, respectively. The warfare escalated further when Johnson decided to abandon Buffalo and instead place a team in Boston, thereby directly challenging the National League in three of its most important cities.

Baseball's newest major league was an immediate success. More than 100 players, and several umpires, went over to the American League. So did the fans; in 1902, the AL outdrew its rival by half a million fans. A peace agreement was finally signed between the two leagues early in 1903. The "National Agreement" acknowledged the American League as a major league, and bound both leagues to respect each other's contracts and reserve lists.

The war between the major leagues had taken a terrible toll on minor league organizations. The Americans and Nationals both openly raided the minors for players to fill their rosters. To protect themselves, the heads of seven minor leagues, including the New England League, Eastern League, and Connecticut League, gathered at the end of the 1901 season to form the National Association of Professional Baseball Leagues. The Association established a minor league classification system in which leagues were classed from "A" (largest) to "D". The system specified minimum population requirements for cities in each class, salary limits for players, and compensation to teams for players drafted by higher leagues. In 1903, the Association signed on to the National Agreement, and organized baseball had the structure that it would maintain for decades.

Refinements to the baseball diamond and the rulebook continued. In 1900, home base was changed from a 12-inch square to the now familiar 17-inch wide, five-sided shape. The infield fly rule was instituted the following year. And for the first time, a foul ball not caught on the fly was counted as a strike unless there were already two strikes on the batter (prior to this, foul balls didn't count as anything). In 1903, the pitcher's mound was limited to 15 inches in height. Starting in 1904, in an effort to speed up the game, the home team was required to give the umpire two baseballs so that there would be an alternate ball available to keep the game going in the event that a foul ball had to be retrieved from the stands (fans were not allowed to keep baseballs until the 1920s). In 1906, players *other than the pitcher* were prohibited from defacing the ball; pitchers were still allowed to load baseballs with everything from tobacco juice to talcum powder to paraffin.

The style of baseball played in the first decade of the twentieth century became known as "inside baseball." Home runs were rare (Tommy Leach won the 1902 National League home run crown with six) and games were generally low-scoring. A winning strategy relied on good pitching, sacrifice bunts, hit-and-run plays, and stolen bases. Some of the game's greatest players made their major-league debuts during the decade, including outfielders Ty Cobb, Joe Jackson, and Tris Speaker; infielders Johnny Evers and Eddie Collins; pitchers Walter Johnson, Christy Mathewson, Eddie Plank, and Three Finger Brown.

By the end of the decade, crowds were coming to the ballparks in greater numbers than ever before. And every fall, in cities throughout the country, people gathered outside newspaper offices to follow the results of the World Series. Baseball was back as the national pastime.

At the turn of the century, the most rabid fan club in baseball was Boston's Royal Rooters, led by Michael "Nuf Ced" McGreevey (so called because his word was the final say on any baseball matter). Headquarters for the Royal Rooters was McGreevey's Third Base Saloon at 940 Columbus Avenue in Roxbury near the South End Grounds. According to the bar's slogan, Third Base should be "the last stop before you steal home." *Above:* The photograph shows the life-sized statue called "The Baseball Man" positioned above the saloon's entrance like the figurehead on the prow of a ship. *Below:* The interior was filled with memorabilia and photographs, and the decor was a baseball fanatic's dream (note the lightbulb "baseballs" suspended from bats). The Royal Rooters began as supporters of the Beaneaters in the 1890s, but when the National League team raised ticket prices in 1901, they switched their allegiance to the new Boston Pilgrims. In 1916, McGreevey moved the Royal Rooters' home base to the corner of Tremont and Ruggles Streets. When Prohibition came a few years later, the Third Base Saloon closed. The building was later used as the Roxbury Crossing branch of the Boston Public Library, and the photographs "Nuf Ced" had accumulated now form the famous McGreevey Collection in the library's Print Department. *Photos courtesy of the Boston Public Library, Print Department.*

Harvard University shortstop William Clarence Matthews (Class of '05) in the Spring of 1903. Matthews had been captain of the baseball team at Phillips Academy in Andover, Massachusetts, before enrolling in Harvard. Several college teams (including Georgetown) refused to take the field with a black ballplayer and demanded that Matthews be benched; Harvard never gave in to those demands, refusing to play without their popular shortstop. While at Harvard, Matthews received national acclaim as one of the best college players in the country. In 1905, after four years with the Crimson, Matthews played professionally with Burlington, Vermont, in the "outlaw" Northern League. His skills were so great that Boston manager Fred Tenney wanted to sign Matthews for his National League club, which would have made Matthews the first African-American major-leaguer in this century. Baseball's color barrier proved impenetrable, however, and Tenney could not get league approval to sign the star short-stop. Matthews left baseball, and obtained a law degree from Boston University, passing the bar exam in 1908. In 1912, President William Taft appointed Matthews assistant to the Massachusetts Attorney General. A dozen years later, Matthews was named an Assistant United States District Attorney by President Calvin Coolidge. *Photo courtesy of Harvard University Archives.*

BOSTON PILGRIMS

Boston's entry into the 1901 American League was unusual in that it wasn't brought about because of demand from local fans, investors, or civic leaders. The driving force behind the franchise was Ban Johnson, who wanted another battleground in a National League market. Financing for the team came from Charles W. Somers, a Cleveland coal magnate.

Somers was instrumental in the growth of the new league. He put up money for four of its eight teams, including his own Cleveland franchise, Boston, Philadelphia, and Chicago. A close friend of Johnson, Somers served as vice president of the American League during its first seventeen years. He was president of the Boston team in its first two years, then became president of the Cleveland club.

A Hub team, called the "Pilgrims" among other names, was quickly assembled, primarily through the acquisition of National League veterans. Jimmy Collins, Chick Stahl, Buck Freeman, and Ted Lewis come over from the Boston Beaneaters, with Collins appointed the club's first manager. The big prize for Boston was pitcher Cy Young, who jumped from St. Louis along with his personal catcher, Lou Criger. Young was thirty-fours years old when he joined the Boston club, and had already notched 286 major-league victories.

The next step was to find a place for the team to play, and again Ban Johnson took charge of the matter. He sent Connie Mack and Boston's former "Heavenly Twins," Hugh Duffy and Tommy McCarthy, to scout locations for a ballpark. They settled on an abandoned circus lot across the railroad tracks from the South End Grounds, on the corner of Huntington and Rogers Avenues. The land was in poor shape for a prospective baseball diamond—among other problems, there was a deep pond that had been used for a "Shoot the Chutes" ride. Nevertheless, ground was broken on March 12, 1901, and construction began. The result was the Huntington Avenue Grounds, the most misshapen ballpark in major-league history. It was only 280 feet down the line in right field, but 530 feet to the fence in centerfield—a distance which was later increased to 635 feet! Playing the outfield was an adventure: not only was there a tremendous amount of ground to cover, but the turf itself was still uneven and dotted with slippery patches of sand from its circus days; there was also a tool shed in center field that was in play.

Less than two months after the groundbreaking, the Boston Pilgrims played their first home game.

It was fitting that the first team to visit Huntington Avenue Grounds was the Philadelphia Athletics. The Athletics were to be involved in some of the most unusual games ever to be played at the park. On August 11, 1903, eccentric Philadelphia pitcher Rube Waddell hit a long foul fly that landed in the steam whistle of a nearby bean cannery; the jammed ball caused a pressure build-up and subsequent explosion that showered the right field bleachers with hot beans. On May 5, 1904, Boston's Cy Young hurled a 3–0 perfect game against Waddell and the Athletics for his second career no-hitter. The next year, on the Fourth of July, Waddell and Young hooked up in a 20-inning pitching duel at the Grounds—a game in which Waddell finally doubled home

May 8, 1901: Auspicious Opening

The Boston American Leaguers started their inaugural season on the road, in Baltimore. It wasn't a promising beginning: after two days of rainouts, Boston lost its first three games. They completed their road trip with a 5–5 record, and returned to Boston barely one hour before the scheduled start of their home opener. The *Boston Herald* reported the following day that the team played on empty stomachs but exhibited "a fine old slugging game":

A HOME VICTORY AT THE NEW GROUNDS
Eleven Thousand See Collins' Team Beat the Athletics, 12 to 4
AUSPICIOUS OPENING
Music and Tally-Hos and a Fine Old Slugging Game—Cy Young Pitches
STAHL BREAKS A RIB

Over 11,000 people yelled themselves hoarse on Huntington avenue yesterday for Jimmy Collins and his American league band and the way they thumped the ball. Evidently, Pitcher Bernhardt, the tall Philadelphian, was not at his best, but the Athletics are not strong in the pitching department just now, and Bernhardt had to stand the pummelling for eight innings. On the other hand, big "Cy" Young was in splendid form, and in but one inning, the eighth, was he found to any extent.

The weather was all the most ardent rooter could desire. By 3 o'clock every seat on the bleachers back of first and third bases was occupied. The Boston Cadet band of 24 pieces gave a splendid concert from 2 o'clock until play was called, and then retired to left field.

An innovation was the appearance of the megaphone man, Charles Moore, who announced the batteries to all parts of the field, and he kept the patrons posted on changes in the teams.

From a partisan standpoint, the game was all that could be desired. Not until the Bostons had rolled up 11 runs and cries were frequent to take Bernhardt out did the visitors succeed in making a run.

As usual, Collins played a grand game at third, and ended in brilliant style by capturing a liner off Geier's bat in his own inimitable style. On his first time at bat he was presented with a basket of gorgeous roses and an immense floral horse shoe.

The work of the new players passed muster successfully. Young Parent showed himself an artist of the first water.

Ferris certainly acquitted himself with great credit, hitting strongly and fielding perfectly. "Buck" Freeman has the honor of making the first home run on the grounds, banging the ball over Geier's head. Another drive to left would have netted him a homer had it not been for ground rules. Freeman played well at first and showed lots of "ginger" in his work.

"Cy" Young not only pitched great ball, but hit well, for the third time this season making two hits in a game. His fielding was a treat. Criger supported him splendidly.

"Chick" Stahl had to retire in favor of Jones when on first in the fourth inning. He complained of a strained side, but it was found that he had fractured a rib. He will be out of the game for 10 days at least.

BOSTON

	ab.	bh.	po.	a.	e.
Dowd, lf	5	3	1	0	0
H'mphill, r	4	4	1	1	0
Stahl, cf	2	1	2	0	0
Jones, cf	2	0	2	0	0
Collins, 3	5	2	1	4	0
Freeman, 1	5	3	10	1	1
Parent, s	5	2	2	1	2
Ferris, 2	5	3	4	2	0
Criger, c	5	2	4	1	0
Young, p	5	2	0	3	0
Totals	43	22	27	10	3

ATHLETICS

	ab.	bh.	po.	a.	e.
Hayden, r	5	2	0	1	2
Geier, cf	5	0	2	0	0
Fultz, lf	4	3	6	1	1
Lajoie, 2	4	3	2	2	0
Seybold, 1	4	2	10	0	0
Cross, 3	4	0	1	6	1
Lockhead, s	4	0	2	2	0
Powers, c	4	0	0	3	1
Bernh'rdt, p	4	1	1	5	0
Totals	38	11	24	20	5

Innings	1	2	3	4	5	6	7	8	9		
Boston	4	1	1	3	2	0	1	0	—	12
Athletics	0	0	0	0	0	0	1	3	0	—	4

Runs earned—Boston 10, Athletics 3. Runs made—Dowd 2, Hemphill 3, Jones, Collins, Freeman, Parent, Ferris, Young 2, Fultz, Lajoie, Seybold, Lockhead. Two-base hit—Hemphill. Three-base hits—Dowd, Hemphill, Freeman, Young, Seybold. Home run—Freeman. Sacrifice hit—Stahl. Stolen bases—Hemphill, Parent, Young, Hayden. First base on balls—Hemphill. First base on errors—Boston 2, Athletics 3. Left on bases—Boston 8, Athletics 6. Struck out—Geier, Bernhardt. Double play—Parent, Ferris and Freeman. Time—2h, 47m. Umpire—Haskell. Attendance—11,025.

the winning run. Philadelphia was again the visiting team on June 27, 1911, when Athletics' first baseman Stuffy McInnis hit a home run on a warmup toss by Boston's Ed Karger; the umpire allowed the homer to stand because, in an effort to speed up games, Ban Johnson had recently banned warmup pitches.

The Boston team that took the field in 1901 remained largely intact for several years. Jimmy Collins did double-duty as third baseman and manager until mid-1906. At first base (and later in the outfield) was Buck Freeman, a slugger who had once led the National League in home runs with 25 (only two shy of the record that would stand until Babe Ruth broke it in 1919). The keystone combination consisted of a couple of New England youngsters: rookie second baseman Hobe Ferris from Providence, and Freddy Parent, a shortstop from Biddeford, Maine, who had only two games of previous big league experience. Catching duties were split between Lou

Boston fans swarming over the Huntington Avenue Base Ball Grounds, October 3, 1903, prior to the start of Game Three of the first modern World Series. It was common practice for fans to be on the playing field in those days, even while the game was in progress. In this photograph, they are also seen occupying every inch of space atop the ballpark's fence. The American League Boston Pilgrims took the series five games to three (the format was best-of-nine) from the Pittsburgh Pirates. One Pittsburgh player later gave credit for the victory to Boston's Royal Rooters and a popular song of the day. When Lawrence Ritter interviewed Tommy Leach for his classic book *The Glory of Their Times,* the former Pirate third baseman told him, "I think those Boston fans actually won that Series for the Red Sox. We beat them three out of the first four games, and then they started singing that damn *Tessie* song . . . you could hardly play ball they were singing *Tessie* so damn loud . . . Sort of got on your nerves after a while. And before we knew what happened, we'd lost the World Series." *Photo courtesy of the Boston Public Library, Print Department.*

Criger, who usually caught when Cy Young pitched, and Ossee Schreckengost, whose name was often abbreviated "Schreck" in box scores. Given the unenviable task of patrolling center field was Chick Stahl, a fine defensive player and .300 hitter. Joining Stahl in the outfield were "Buttermilk Tommy" Dowd, who played briefly on Boston's 1891 American Association team, and Charlie "Eagle Eye" Hemphill (in his only year of major-league ball prior to 1901, Hemphill had a dreadful fielding average of .837, so presumably his nickname was not in reference to his ability to spot fly balls). The mainstays of the pitching staff were Cy Young, Ted Lewis, and rookie George "Sassafras" Winter.

While the line-up was relatively stable, a nickname for the team wasn't finalized for years. Usually called the "Pilgrims," and often simply the "Americans," the club was also widely known as the "Somersets," after its benefactor Charles Somers. In its early years, the Boston American Leaguers were also called the "Puritans" and the "Plymouth

Rocks." The name "Red Sox" wasn't officially adopted until December, 1907. Boston's National League team had stopped wearing red socks that year because the dye sometimes caused infections when players were spiked; the American Leaguers—apparently unconcerned about such injuries—promptly added red stockings to their own uniform design.

After its first home stand, Boston continued to play strong, and quickly moved into first place. With Cy Young winning 12 consecutive games, and Buck Freeman and Jimmy Collins among the league leaders in hitting, the team remained at the top of the standings as late as July 17. Thereafter, the pitching started to collapse, and the Pilgrims struggled. The team ended the season in second place, behind the Chicago White Sox. Cy Young's individual achievements were remarkable: he led both major leagues in wins (33) and earned run average (1.62), and led the American League in strikeouts and shutouts.

The team was strengthened in 1902 by the addition of veteran first baseman Candy LaChance, of Waterbury, Connecticut, and pitcher "Big Bill" Dinneen, who jumped to the American League from the Beaneaters. Rookie Patsy Dougherty made his major-league debut in the outfield, and went on to lead the team in batting with a .342 average. A four-way battle for the title was fought through most of the season; when it ended, Boston had to settle for third place. Cy Young again dominated the league in pitching, though, chalking up 32 wins, while Bill Dinneen notched 21 victories.

1903 was the first year under the peace agreement with the National League, and it was to be an historic season. Aided by pitcher Long Tom Hughes, who'd joined the team late in 1902, Boston ran away with the title, ending up 14 1/2 games ahead of second-place Philadelphia. Cy Young led the league with 28 wins, while Bill Dinneen and Tom Hughes had 21 and 20, respectively. Buck Freeman led in home runs (13) and RBIs, and Patsy Dougherty had the most hits and runs in the league.

Partly in an attempt to heal the rift between the two leagues, the Boston Pilgrims and the National League champion Pittsburgh Pirates agreed to a postseason best-of-nine series to determine the "World's Champion." The first modern World Series game was played in Boston's Huntington Avenue Grounds on October 1, 1903. The results were a disappointment to the thousands of fans who jammed the stands and crowded onto the field itself. Cy Young gave up four runs in the first inning, and suffered a 7–3 defeat. Boston evened the series with a 3–0 win the following day; Bill Dinneen struck out 11 batters in hurling the shutout, and Patsy Dougherty hit two home runs. Pittsburgh then took the next two games for a commanding 3–1 lead in the series. Cheered on by their Royal Rooters, however, the American Leaguers won the next four games in a row, to take the series five games to three. The final game was another 3–0 shutout pitched by Bill Dinneen (his third win of the series) in Boston. On October 13, 1903, the Boston Pilgrims were crowned World's Champions.

In 1904, *Boston Globe* publisher Charles Taylor purchased the ballclub, and named his son John I. Taylor president (it was said at the time that the elder Taylor had bought the club to give his son a hobby).

The first year under Taylor's control turned out to be another one for the history books. After the 1902 season, the American League's Baltimore franchise had moved to

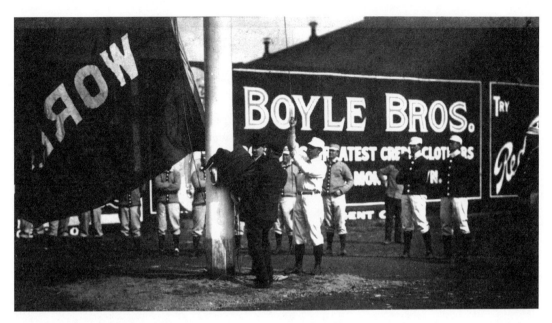

Above: Opening Day, 1904, at Huntington Avenue Grounds. Boston Pilgrims manager Jimmy Collins raises the 1903 World Championship banner. The Pilgrims went on to repeat as American League champions in 1904, but the New York Giants refused to play them in a World Series. *Photo courtesy of the Boston Public Library, Print Department.* *Below:* Opening Day, 1904, in Lowell, Massachusetts. At the same time that Boston was celebrating its World Championship of the previous season, the New England League Championship banner being raised in Lowell. The 1903 pennant was the city's first since 1888. *Photo courtesy of the Boston Public Library, Print Department.*

New York, where it became known as the Highlanders (later to be called the Yankees). In 1904, Boston and New York fought their first battle for an American League pennant. All season, the two teams dueled it out for first place. One of those helping the Boston cause was pitcher Jesse Tannehill who'd been on the New York staff the year before; Tannehill contributed 21 wins, including a no-hitter, to the Boston victory column. New York pitcher "Happy Jack" Chesbro completely dominated the American League in 1904, however, setting a twentieth century record with 41 wins.

The season came down to the last day, October 10, a doubleheader between Boston and the Highlanders in New York's Hilltop Park. Jack Chesbro pitched the first game for New York and held the Pilgrims to a 2–2 tie into the ninth inning; then, with two outs and a runner on third base, Chesbro unleashed a wild pitch that allowed the winning run to score. Boston had won its second American League pennant in a row. But there was to be no World Series. John McGraw, manager of the National League champion New York Giants (McGraw had jumped back to the senior league after only a year and a half with the junior circuit), hated American League president Ban Johnson and refused to play the champions of what he called a "minor league."

Boston's fortunes soon started to decline. The team dropped to fifth place in 1905 and finished in the cellar the following year. Chick Stahl replaced his friend Jimmy Collins as manager in the final month of the 1906 season, and was to continue in that capacity in 1907; during spring training, however, Stahl committed suicide by drinking carbolic acid.

The Boston American Leaguers went through four managers in 1907, including Cy Young and Deacon McGuire, on their way to a seventh-place finish. The team, now known as the "Red Sox," would not win another pennant while playing at the Huntington Avenue Grounds.

VERMONT LEAGUES

In 1902, St. Albans, Vermont, entered the Northern New York League as a replacement team. Since the league was a signatory to the National Agreement, this marked the first appearance of a Vermont franchise in organized baseball.

That status was to be short-lived: at the close of the season, the teams couldn't agree on the final standings, and the league ceased to exist in its original form. St. Albans and Plattsburgh, New York, remained, and were joined by Burlington and Rutland, which had been the largest cities in the Western Vermont League. Together, the four teams organized the "outlaw" Northern League of 1903.

In several ways, the league lived up to the "outlaw" name. The president of the St. Albans club was Jack Thompson, a saloon keeper and gambler (at the time, St. Albans was a summer resort with a permissive attitude toward gambling). Another gambler, millionaire horse breeder George Whitney, purchased the Burlington team in 1904. Gambling was a major problem for the circuit, and even league president J. B. White was accused of betting on games. In addition to gambling, the league was plagued by contract-jumping, the use of ringers, and episodes of player drunkenness.

New York Highlander pitcher Jack Chesbro was one of the ringers hired to pitch a

The Northern League's 1903 St. Albans team with manager Arthur "Punch" Daley (in bow tie). The club's two-man pitching rotation consisted of Bob Dresser (front row, center) and Buck O'Brien (back row, right). Dresser had pitched—and lost—one game for the Boston National Leaguers the year before in what would be his only major-league appearance. Buck O'Brien would later pitch for the Boston Red Sox, winning 19 games for the 1912 World Champions. *Photo courtesy of the St. Albans Historical Society.*

Northern League game in 1903. Rutland brought him from New York on an over-night train to pitch for the Vermont team on July 9. Unfortunately for Rutland fans, Chesbro spent the train ride drinking and was unable to take the mound. He instead played outfield, while his brother Dan (who appeared to be in a similar condition) stepped in to pitch. Dan Chesbro didn't last long; according to the Rutland *Daily Herald*, "He got in some fine target practice. Hitting the first three Plattsburgh batters, but failing to kill any of them, he retired from the box." Ironically, Rutland won the game anyway, aided by a double from Jack Chesbro's bat. Chesbro promptly returned to New York, where he posted his third straight 20-win season.

A fifth team was added to the Northern League in 1904: Barre-Montpelier (the team became known as the "Hyphens"), under the ownership of former St. Albans manager Arthur "Punch" Daley. The strength of the league is evidenced by the fact that thirty of its players from the 1904 season went on to play in the majors.

Despite fielding some excellent ballplayers, the Northern League was not finan-cially profitable. The league struggled along into 1906. Indicative of the league's problems, Plattsburgh didn't have a team together by opening day and so was represented by the local high school squad in the season's first game (although when Plattsburgh finally did assemble a roster, it briefly included future Hall-of-Famer Eddie Collins in his professional debut). By the end of the year, attrition had left Burlington and Barre-Montpelier carrying on as a two-team "league." After Burlington claimed the 1906 pennant, the league collapsed.

While it existed, the Northern League featured some of the best players in New England, including many college stars and future professionals. Jack Coombs, who'd been the pitching ace for Colby College in Waterville, Maine, began his professional career with Barre-Montpelier in 1905; he jumped to the Philadelphia Athletics the next year, and in 1910 led the major leagues in victories with 31. Starring for St. Albans in 1904 and the Hyphens in 1905, was third baseman "Harvard Eddie" Grant, from Franklin, Massachusetts; Grant jumped to the big leagues later in 1905 and went on to a ten-year career in the majors (sadly, he is best known for being killed in action in World War I). In a league dominated by pitching, "Big Ed" Reulbach was one of the best; he went undefeated for Barre-Montpelier in 1904 while studying at the University of Vermont in Burlington; the next year, he became a mainstay of the Chicago Cubs pitching staff and won 182 games during a 13-year big-league career. Lefty George pitched for St. Albans in 1904 and Plattsburgh in 1905; George later played parts of four seasons in the big leagues, posting a lifetime record of 7–21; he continued to pitch minor league ball for decades, making his last professional appearance in 1944 at age 57 and totaling 327 career wins in the minors. Another college star to appear in the Northern League was African-American shortstop William Clarence Matthews from Harvard; because of baseball's color line, his only professional appearances were with Burlington in 1905. A member of the 1905 Plattsburgh team had to wait the longest to achieve fame: Archibald "Moonlight" Graham, best known from the movie *Field of Dreams*.

In Franklin County, Vermont, bordered by Quebec to the north and Lake Champlain to the west, another league was formed in 1905. The Franklin County League included teams from Enosburg Falls, Richford, and St. Albans, which had recently dropped out of the Northern League because of heavy financial losses. While St. Albans still had a strong roster, Enosburg Falls and Richford also boasted talented teams. Starring for Enosburg Falls was 17-year-old pitcher Larry Gardner, who later became a third baseman with the Boston Red Sox, and played almost 2,000 major league games in seventeen years. Pitching for Richford was one of the town's most colorful characters, "Whiskey Jack" Bishop; Bishop, a heavy drinker, had been a southern hobo who remained in Richford after being thrown off a train. Richford, behind Bishop's superb pitching, won the pennant in the league's only year of existence.

After the Northern League folded in 1906, the two teams that had survived that season—Burlington and Barre-Montpelier—searched for another league to join. Both were admitted to the 1907 New Hampshire League, a Class D minor league with franchises in Concord, Franklin, Laconia, Nashua, East Manchester, and West Manchester. The Northern League veterans so dominated their competition that four of the New Hampshire teams folded within the first three weeks of the season. After a few more franchise changes, the association was renamed the "Vermont League" and was

July 31, 1904: Jake Volz's Day For Sure

Jake Volz was one of those players who toiled for years in the minor leagues, with only a few appearances in the big leagues. After winning one game in his sole appearance for the 1901 Boston Pilgrims (he pitched the last game of the season, and despite walking nine batters, held on for a 10–9 victory), he was back in the New England League. On July 31, 1904, while pitching for sixth-place Manchester, New Hampshire, he achieved a feat that was remarkable in any league. As reported in the *Manchester Union*:

JAKE VOLZ'S DAY FOR SURE
Had Nashua Trimmed All the Time
HE WON TWO GREAT GAMES

Manchester took both games of a double-header with Nashua Saturday afternoon at Varick park, winning the first by a score of 3 to 0, and the second, 3 to 1. Both games were stubborn contests and the way the locals played was a revelation.

To Jake Volz belong the honors of the day, for he pitched both games and his twirling has never been equalled in this city. It was nothing short of phenomenal. Five hits in both games was all the visitors could do with his delivery. Volz gave but two bases on balls, both of which were in the first game.

Twelve of the Nashua heavy hitters were struck out in both games. By winning both games from Nashua Volz made a record for the week. On Thursday he pitched against Fall River and shut them out, 3 to 0. During that game he struck out fifteen men and allowed but one hit.

In the three games for the week Volz struck out twenty-seven men in as many innings, allowed but six hits, only one of which was for extra bases, and gave but four bases on balls—a record which probably will stand.

There was a good attendance and the crowd got its money's worth. Several Nashua rooters were present and they did not take kindly to the two defeats. As for the home fans, it is needless to say that they were well satisfied.

Rollins and Merritt were the battery for the visitors in the first game.

The score:

MANCHESTER	ab.	r.	bh.	po.	a.	e.
Graham, cf	4	1	1	0	0	0
Armbuster, lf	4	1	2	3	0	0
Smith, rf	4	0	0	1	0	0
Warren, 3b	4	1	1	1	3	0
Chapman, 1b	4	0	1	5	0	1
Taylor, 2b	4	0	1	1	1	0
Knau, ss	3	0	0	2	3	1

NASHUA	ab.	r.	bh.	po.	a.	e.
Pastor, ss	4	0	0	0	5	2
Van Zant, cf	4	0	1	3	0	0
Wilson, 3b	4	0	0	1	2	0
Cassidy, lf	4	0	0	1	0	0
Merritt, c	2	0	0	4	2	0
Birmingham, 1b	3	0	0	12	0	0
Labelle, rf	3	0	1	0	0	0

	ab.	r.	bh.	po.	a.	e.			ab.	r.	bh.	po.	a.	e.
Page, c	3	0	1	14	0	0		Southwell, 2b	3	0	0	2	3	0
Volz, p	3	0	0	0	2	0		Rollins, p	3	0	0	1	1	0
Totals	33	3	7	27	9	2		Totals	30	0	2	24	13	2

Innings	1	2	3	4	5	6	7	8	9		
Manchester	3	0	0	0	0	0	0	0		—	3
Nashua	0	0	0	0	0	0	0	0	0	—	0

Stolen bases—Armbuster 2, Warren. Left on bases—Manchester, 6; Nashua, 4. First base on balls—Off Volz, 2. Struck out—By Volz, 7; by Rollins, 4. Time—1:45. Umpire—Kerins. Attendance—1,200.

When Umpire Kerins announced that Volz and Page would continue as the battery for the home team in the second game, the crowd sent up a mighty cheer, for it was anxious to see the visitors get a sound trimming, and they did.

The score:

MANCHESTER

NASHUA

	ab.	r.	bh.	po.	a.	e.			ab.	r.	bh.	po.	a.	e.
Graham, cf	4	1	0	2	0	0		Pastor, ss	4	0	2	1	4	0
Armbuster, lf	4	1	2	3	0	0		Van Zant, cf	3	1	1	2	1	0
Smith, rf	4	0	2	0	0	0		Wilson, 3b	4	0	0	1	2	0
Warren, 3b	4	0	2	0	0	1		Cassidy, lf	3	0	0	3	0	0
Chapman, 1b	4	1	3	9	1	1		Duggan, c	3	0	0	8	0	1
Taylor, 2b	4	0	2	3	6	0		Birmingham, 1b	2	0	0	6	0	1
Knau, ss	4	0	0	3	4	0		Labelle, rf	3	0	0	0	0	1
Page, c	3	0	2	7	0	0		Southwell, 2b	3	0	0	3	1	0
Volz, p	4	0	0	0	1	0		Gokey, p	3	0	0	0	1	0
Totals	35	3	13	27	12	2		Totals	28	1	3	24	9	3

Innings	1	2	3	4	5	6	7	8	9		
Manchester	0	1	0	0	0	0	2	0		—	3
Nashua	0	0	0	0	0	0	1	0	0	—	1

Earned runs—Manchester, 1. Two-base hits—Smith, Van Zant, Page. Sacrifice hit—Van Zant. Stolen bases—Graham, Knau, Van Zant, Page. Double plays—Taylor, Knau and Chapman; Pastor and Birmingham. Left on bases—Manchester, 7; Nashua, 2. First base on balls—Off Gokey, 1. Struck out—By Volz, 5; by Gokey, 5. Wild pitch—Volz. Hit by pitched ball—Birmingham. Time—1:35. Umpire—Kerins. Attendance—1,200.

The next year, Volz was given a chance with the National League Boston club, but was dropped after posting a 0-and-2 record in three games. His next, and final, appearance in the majors came in 1908, when he picked up his second big-league win, in compiling a lifetime major-league record of two wins and four losses. It had taken him seven years to win the same number of games in the big leagues as he won on July 31, 1904, in the New England League

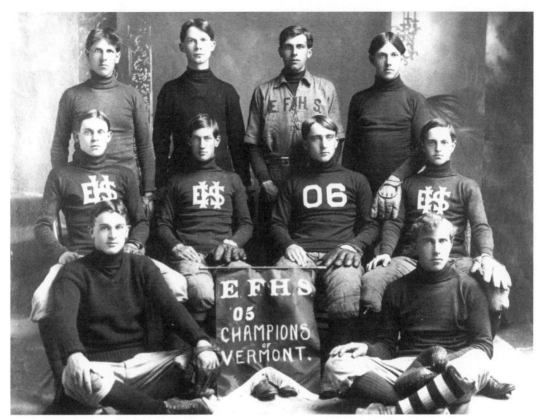

The Enosburg Falls High School baseball team that took the Vermont state championship in 1905. Larry Gardner (lower left) was the team's pitching star; that summer, local newspapers dubbed him the "child marvel" as he competed against older players in the semi-professional Franklin County League. Switching to the infield, Gardner played the next two summers for Burlington in the Northern and Vermont Leagues while a student at the University of Vermont. Following his junior year, he signed with the Boston Red Sox and made his major-league debut in 1908; he then went back to campus and graduated with the Class of 1909. During his seventeen-year big league career, Gardner established himself as one of the best third basemen in the game. He played in four World Series, and it was Larry Gardner who drove in the run that won the 1912 Series for Boston. He later returned to the University of Vermont as baseball coach and athletic director. *Photo courtesy of Enosburg Historical Society.*

almost an exact copy of the former Northern League, with teams in Barre-Montpelier, Burlington, Rutland, and Plattsburgh. Burlington collapsed soon after the league reorganized, and was replaced by the University of Vermont team, which featured Larry Gardner and future major-league pitcher Ray Collins (Gardner made his big-league debut with the Red Sox in 1908; Collins joined him on the Boston club a year later). Barre-Montpelier was leading the Vermont League when it folded at the end of July. It would be four years until professional baseball was again played in the state.

BEANEATERS TO DOVES TO RUSTLERS

The first decade of the twentieth century was a bleak one for Boston's National League team. After a third-place finish in 1902, the club didn't rise higher than sixth for the

1906 game action between the New York Giants and the Boston Beaneaters (the next year, they would become known as the "Doves") in the third construction of South End Grounds. Giants' manager John McGraw is in the third base coach's box. *Photo courtesy of Michael Gershman.*

next ten years. While the American League Pilgrims burst on to the Boston baseball scene as immediate contenders, the Beaneaters found themselves struggling to attract fans and attention.

Even during their best year of the decade, 1902, the Beaneaters were eclipsed by Cy Young, Jimmy Collins, and the other players across the railroad tracks in Huntington Avenue Grounds. Part of the problem was that the old Beaneater favorites were almost all gone. Only three players remained from their pennant-winning 1898 team: Fred Tenney, Herman Long, and Vic Willis. Frank Selee, who had managed the club from 1890 to 1901 was also gone, having been replaced by Al Buckenberger, whose last attempt at managing a major-league club had been in 1895 when he led St. Louis to an eleventh place finish in the twelve-team National League. The Beaneaters' respectable showing in 1902 was largely due to two pitchers, Vic Willis and Togie Pittinger, each of whom won 27 games. Hitting was weak, with Fred Tenney the only one to bat higher than .300.

In 1903, the year the Pilgrims won the first modern World Series, the Boston Beaneaters slipped to sixth place. They'd lost Herman Long to the American League, stalwart Vic Willis managed to win only a dozen games, and Togie Pittinger, who'd been such a pleasant surprise the year before, led the league in losses with 22. One of the few highlights of 1903 was a 3–2 win over the Philadelphia Phillies on September 6; because the South End Grounds were temporarily unavailable, the contest took place in Rocky Point Park in Warwick, Rhode Island—the only major-league game to be played in a ballpark where the entire outfield was surrounded by ocean (home runs ended up in Narragansett Bay).

Oct. 9, 1905: Tenney's Boys Spring a Huge Surprise

In 1903, at the same time that the Boston Pilgrims were facing Pittsburgh in the first modern World Series, several cities that had franchises in both the National and American leagues staged post-season series between their hometown clubs. Among them were Chicago, Philadelphia, and St. Louis; there was also an Ohio series between Cincinnati and Cleveland. Boston held its first city series in 1905, when neither of its teams was in contention for a league championship. The American Leaguers finished their season in fourth place, and the Beaneaters were a dismal seventh in the National League, more than 50 games behind the pennant winners. The opening game of the Hub series was played on October 9, and the National Leaguers scored an upset, as described in the *Boston Globe*:

TENNEY'S BOYS SPRING A HUGE SURPRISE.
Willis Proves Too Much for Collins' Team, With Dineen In the Box.
BOSTON NATIONALS WIN.

Outclassing their opponents in every department of the game, and playing better ball than they have at any stage of the past season, the Boston Nationals scored a 5 to 2 victory over the Boston Americans in the opening contest of the postseason series at the Huntington-av grounds yesterday afternoon.

At the bat and in the field, on the bases and in headwork, the Nationals loomed up strong and the lead secured in the first inning was never lost by Tenney's boys.

More than 7100 enthusiastic followers of the game gathered to cheer the rivals on in their tussle for supremacy.

The outcome of the initial contest was a big surprise and considerable money changed hands. The betting was at odds of 10 to 5 and several bets were made at 10 to 4.

Capt Tenney put in Vic Willis to face the American leaguers, and Capt Collins relied on Bill Dineen to pull off the victory for his team.

Weird fielding stunts contributed by Burkett and Bill Dineen figured in the victory secured by Tenney's men. In the left garden Burkett allowed Cosey [sic] Dolan's single to get away from him and roll to the fence in the sixth inning, giving Dolan a trip to third, from where he scored a minute later on Delehanty's single. In the ninth Dineen dropped Wolverton's easy pop fly. Cannell followed with a sharp single and after Raymer had flied to Grimshaw, Moran lined the ball to left field. Burkett badly misjudged the hit and in an effort to get the ball while running backward, turned a complete somerset [sic], allowing Wolverton and Cannell to tally and Moran to reach third base, from where he trotted home on a fly to left by Willis.

Cannell's fielding was the feature of the game. In the second inning Burkett slammed a long, low liner toward the bleachers in left centerfield, but Cannell ran back for it fast and got it while sprinting at top speed and going in the direction of the ball's flight. Stahl gave Cannell another opportunity to distinguish himself in the sixth inning, and this time he got the ball by a pretty dive, rolling over after the catch.

The heaviest hitting was done by Moran and Selbach. The former had a single, double and triple to his credit, and Selbach two singles and a double. Delehanty, Cannell and Grimshaw got two singles.

The score:

BOST N L	AB	R	BH	TB	PO	A	E		AMERICANS	AB	R	BH	TB	PO	A	E
Abbaticchio, ss	4	1	0	0	3	3	0		Parent, ss	4	0	0	0	1	3	0
Tenney, 1b	4	0	1	1	10	0	1		Stahl, cf	3	0	0	0	1	0	0
Dolan, rf	3	1	1	1	0	0	0		Unglaub, 3b	3	0	0	0	0	2	0
Delehanty, lf	4	0	2	2	0	0	0		Burkett, lf	4	1	1	3	3	0	1
Wolverton, 3b	3	1	0	0	1	1	0		Grimshaw, 1b	4	1	2	2	12	0	0
Cannell, cf	4	1	2	2	3	0	0		Selbach, rf	3	0	3	4	2	0	0
Raymer, 2b	3	0	0	0	2	1	0		Ferris, 2b	4	0	1	1	2	1	1
Moran, c	4	1	3	6	8	3	1		Criger, c	3	0	0	0	4	1	0
Willis, p	4	0	0	0	0	6	0		Dineen, p	2	0	0	0	2	4	1
Totals	33	5	9	12	27	14	2		*Freeman	1	0	0	0	0	0	0
									Totals	49	2	7	10	27	11	3

* Batted for Dineen in ninth

Innings	1	2	3	4	5	6	7	8	9		
Nationals	1	0	0	0	0	1	0	0	3	—	5
Americans	0	0	0	0	0	0	1	0	1	—	2

Two-base hits, Selbach, Moran. Three-base hits, Moran, Burkett. Stolen base, Abbaticchio. Sacrifice hits, Raymer, Wolverton, Dineen. First base on balls, Parent, Stahl, Unglaub, Selbach, Criger, Abbaticchio, Dolan. Struck out, Tenney, Moran, Unglaub 2, Burkett, Grimshaw, Ferris, Dineen. Double plays, Moran and Raymer; Dineen and Grimshaw. Time 1h 45m. Umpires, O'Loughlin and Johnstone. Attendance 7,108.

This was to be the National's only victory ever in a Boston city series. The Pilgrims swept the next six games to take the 1905 series. A city championship series was next played in 1907, and the American Leaguers won in six straight games. Because fans quickly lost interest, it was the last such series to be played in Boston.

The Beaneaters dropped another notch in 1904; three of their pitchers lost more than 20 games, with Vic Willis's 25 leading the league in that dubious category.

Al Buckenberger was fired after his third season, and Fred Tenney was named manager for 1905. Although the team again came in seventh under Tenney's direction, there was a ray of hope for the future: rookie pitcher Irv Young. In his first season, with a low-scoring team that finished 54 1/2 games out of first place (while the Giants scored 780 runs during the season, Boston's total of 468 was the lowest in either league), Young managed to win 20 games. Comparisons with the Young who pitched for Boston's American League club were inevitable, and Irv was quickly tagged "Young Cy" and "Cy the Second." 1905 was the highlight of Cy the Second's career, though; he won only 43 more games in the big leagues. The season was Vic Willis's last with Boston; after setting an all-time major-league record with 29 losses, he was mercifully sold to Pittsburgh (where he won more than 20 games a season the next four years in a row).

The Beaneaters struck bottom in 1906, losing more than 100 games on their way to a last-place finish 66 1/2 games behind the pennant winners. The pitching staff divvied up the suffering evenly, with four of them each losing more than 20 games.

The club had new ownership in 1907. George and John Dovey bought the team and for a few years it was nicknamed the "Doves" in the brothers' honor. Along with new owners, Boston had a new centerfielder: Ginger Beaumont, who had three times led the National League in hits and was a veteran of three pennant-winning Pittsburgh teams. Fred Tenney remained as manager and first baseman. He was offered a bonus if the team made a profit, and reportedly would go into the stands himself to retrieve baseballs from fans who didn't want to give them back.

Beaumont performed as well as had been hoped in his first season with Boston, batting .322 and leading the league in hits. The only other highlight for the team in 1907, however, was a May 8 no-hitter pitched by "Big Jeff" Pfeffer, who won a paltry six games all year (oddly, Pfeffer had a younger brother also called Jeff who became a major-league pitcher—and the younger Pfeffer was two inches taller than "Big Jeff").

After another seventh-place finish in 1907, Fred Tenney was fired as manager. His replacement was Cambridge native Joe Kelley, former outfielder with the Baltimore Orioles of the 1890s and future Hall-of-Famer. Dan McGann, who had played first base for the both the Orioles and the Beaneaters in the previous decade, also joined the team, as did shortstop "Bad Bill" Dahlen, a 38-year-old veteran of more than 2,000 big-league games.

With Kelley managing and filling in at first base and in the outfield, the Doves did slightly better in 1908, finishing in sixth place. It was to be Kelley's and McGann's final years in the big leagues, however, and Bill Dahlen's last full season as a player.

In 1909, Boston began a streak of four straight last place finishes in the National League. At the end of the next season, the Dovey brothers sold the ballclub to W. Hepburn Russell, and the new owner's name inspired a new nickname for the team: the Rustlers.

MAINE LEAGUES

The lowest minor-league classification in organized baseball was Class D. At this level, there was no minimum population requirement for cities to enter a franchise, team salaries were limited to $700 per month, and no individual player could receive more than $75 a month. A player in Class D could be drafted by a higher level team for a payment of $100 to his former club.

Forty-one-year old Cy Young warming up in 1908. The winningest pitcher in baseball history, Young was the mainstay of the Boston staff from the team's birth in 1901 through 1908. In his eight years with the Red Sox, he won 192 games, including a no-hitter against the Yankees and a perfect game against Rube Waddell and the Philadelphia Athletics. Young returned to Boston in 1911, to close out his career with the Boston Braves; his final win that year gave him 511 victories in his 22-year career. *Photo courtesy of the Library of Congress.*

The Maine State League, which had disbanded after the 1898 season, reorganized in 1907 with Class D status. Teams included Augusta, Bangor, Biddeford, Pine Tree (South Portland), Portland, and Waterville. Augusta and Waterville dropped out before the end of the season, as did Manchester, New Hampshire, which briefly came into the league as a mid-season replacement.

Bangor won the championship, led by its slugging first baseman Fred "Biddo" Iott (also known as "Happy") from Houlton, Maine. Iott was one of the most experienced players in the league; in 1902, he'd been with Concord, New Hampshire, in the New England League, and even made it to the majors for a few games in 1903. He was described by the *Bangor News* as "the one and only 'Biddo' Iott, the great Aroostook player, known far and wide as a heavy hitter and all 'round expert at the game."

Low attendance was a serious problem for the Maine State League in 1908. At various times during the season, there were teams representing Augusta, Bangor, Biddeford, Lewiston, Pine Tree, Portland, and York Beach. When the season ended,

Aug. 30, 1907: Bangor Took a Fine Game

Bangor's final home game of the 1907 season was played at Maplewood Park where a local fair was in progress. The newspaper account of the game mentions a few unusual features of the grounds, including an airship tent and a judges' stand. According to the *Bangor Daily Commercial*, spectators were treated to a thrilling game:

WON IN THE TENTH
Bangor Took a Fine Game From the Portland Blue Sox
THE BEST OF THE SERIES

One of the best exhibitions of baseball the Bangor fans have seen this summer was the last game of the fair series played at Maplewood, Friday afternoon—and, by the way, the last league game Bangor fans will see this season.

Collins was on the slab again for Bangor, although he had pitched the morning game. For the first few innings the Blue Sox had considerable fun with the Green Mountaineer's delivery but after that he steadied down to his winning gait and not a Blue Sox crossed the plate after the fourth.

Big Jack Fraser, the Holy Cross star, tossed 'em over for Portland. Fraser had speed to give away and perfect control. He fanned nine of the Bangor stickers and with a little better support on the part of his infield should have won his game. The Portland infield, by the way, seemed very dopey at times, letting lots of chances for double plays and the like go by them.

Portland drew first blood, scoring in the second on a triple by Barrows and a passed ball. Bangor took the lead in her half, however, on a hit by Covey and a corking home run drive which rolled through the gate onto the track back of center by McMillan.

In the third Fraser tried hard to win his game by a drive over Covey's head. It might not have been good for four bases then, but the ball rolled under the canvas of the airship tent and Fraser simply ambled home. Hits by Breen and Follansbee netted another run and in the fourth "Cuke" Barrows connected for another three-sacker, scoring on the throw-in of Grow's long fly.

With the weak end of the batting order up it looked as if it was all over in the ninth and the Portland fielders got their mitts and things together. There was a surprise waiting for them, however. Fraser passed Finnemore a straight one, swift as a bullet. As the Portland players told Fraser afterward, Finnemore can kill speed and he did this time. The ball stopped in the tall grass back of Barrows and a speedy man would have stretched it into a four sacker, but Finnemore stopped on third, which was a safe way to play it when "Cuke" had the ball. Collins had not been hitting any to speak of but he smashed out a pretty single and the score was tied.

Portland went in for the tenth and stayed just long enough for three men to get out. Iott was first up for Bangor and cracked one to Pinkerton, which the little fellow handled neatly, retiring Iott at first. Gardner pasted one which hit the ground just in front of the plate and bounded high in the air. It was Fraser's ball easy and he got it, but Follansbee went after it too, leaving the bag uncovered, and Gardner was safe by a mile. Then McMillan drove one at Pinkerton and "Pinky" threw the ball to a friend of his out toward the judges' stand. That settled it. It was hard luck for Jack Fraser to have his game lost that way.

The summary:

BANGOR

	AB	R	BH	PO	A	E
Jones, c. f.	5	0	0	3	0	0
Connors, 2b	5	0	0	0	3	0
Iott, 1b	5	0	1	13	0	0
Gardner, 3b	5	2	2	0	2	0
Covey, r. f.	5	1	2	5	0	0
McMillan, l. f.	5	1	2	4	0	0
Finnemore, ss	3	1	1	1	6	0
Monahan, c	4	0	0	4	0	1
Collins, p	4	0	2	0	0	0
Totals	41	5	10	30	11	1

PORTLAND

	AB	R	BH	PO	A	E
Roper, 3b	5	0	0	0	2	1
Breen, l. f.	5	1	1	3	0	0
Follansbee, 1b	4	0	2	8	0	0
Murphy, r. f.	4	0	1	3	0	0
Barrows, c. f.	4	2	2	5	0	0
Pinkerton, ss	4	0	0	0	2	1
Kelley, c	3	0	0	9	1	1
Grow, 2b	4	0	0	1	2	0
Fraser, p	4	1	1	0	0	0
Totals	37	4	7	29★	7	3

★*Winning run with two out.*

Innings	1	2	3	4	5	6	7	8	9	10		
Bangor	0	2	0	0	0	1	0	0	1	1	—	5
Portland	0	1	2	1	0	0	0	0	0	0	—	4

Three base hits, Gardner, Finnemore, Follansbee, Barrows 2. Home runs, McMillan, Fraser. Stolen bases, Covey, McMillan, Breen, Murray. Struck out by Collins 4, by Fraser 9. Passed ball, Monahan. Time 1:40. Umpire, Hasmett.

The season ended four days later. Bangor was crowned champion of the Maine State League, with Biddeford coming in second.

only three teams remained. Portland, which had already clinched the pennant, disbanded with but one week left to play, and Bangor claimed a second championship in the league's final year.

In 1909, Maine teams participated in two leagues. One was the Northern Maine League (usually called the "Potato League"), with clubs in Bangor, Houlton, Millinocket, and Old Town; Bangor transferred to Caribou near the end of the season, and Millinocket won the championship. In southern Maine, Pine Tree and Portland joined with Dover and Somersworth, New Hampshire, to form the Twin State League. Neither the Northern Maine League nor the Twin State League lasted more than the one season, and it was to be several years before Maine was again to field a professional baseball team.

BOSTON RED SOX

Boston's American League club started the 1908 season with a new name, and during the course of the year began to assemble a new roster that would soon evolve into one of the greatest teams in baseball history.

Before the season started, however, the Red Sox nearly lost the player who would become its star center fielder. During the last two weeks of the 1907 campaign, Tris Speaker, a 19-year-old former cowpuncher from Texas, made his big-league debut with Boston, playing in seven games. Speaker hit only .158 in those games, and was not offered a contract for the next year. He showed up at spring training camp in Little Rock, Arkansas, anyway, where the Red Sox allowed him to practice with the team. They then gave him to Little Rock's minor league club as payment for using their park! Speaker was batting .350 for Little Rock when Boston bought him back; he played 31 games for the Red Sox in 1908, and remained in the big leagues until 1928, playing in 2,789 games and totaling 3,514 base hits with a .345 lifetime average (he probably remains the only player ever to be traded for a practice field).

Catcher Bill "Rough" Carrigan was given another chance with Red Sox in 1908. The Lewiston, Maine native had played in 37 games for the team in 1906, but his .211 batting average had him back in the minors for the 1907 season. Carrigan would spend his entire ten-year playing career with the Red Sox, and manage the club for seven years.

Another addition to the team was knuckleball pitcher Eddie Cicotte. His entire major-league career before joining the Red Sox in 1908 consisted of a three-game stint with the 1905 Detroit Tigers. Cicotte was a reliable, though unexceptional, pitcher for Boston until his 1912 sale to the Chicago White Sox (with whom he would gain notoriety for helping to throw the 1919 World Series).

Several other players joined the club after the season got under way. Jake Stahl, who'd been a part-time catcher on Boston's 1903 championship team, came to the Red Sox from New York to play first base. Larry Gardner, the pride of Enosburg Falls, Vermont, made his major-league debut on June 25; he played only three games in 1908, but soon became the team's regular third baseman. Young pitcher Smokey Joe Wood made his debut on August 24; within a few years, he would be the outstanding hurler in the American League.

A new manager was also hired in August of 1908. Fred Lake, a Canadian who had played briefly for the Beaneaters in 1891 and 1897, replaced Deacon McGuire at the helm.

The changes that had been made were yet to produce winning results, however. Despite the new additions, and the continuing development of young players like shortstop Heinie Wagner, the Red Sox ended the 1908 season in fifth place.

The Boston Bloomer Girls, one of several women's professional barnstorming baseball teams that toured throughout the United States and Canada, lasted for more than thirty years. In 1892 and 1893, the Boston Bloomer Girls toured the country with another women's team, the New York Champions. Later, the club played almost exclusively against men. During a 26-day period in 1903, the Bloomer Girls won 28 games against men's teams with no defeats. A star attraction for the team was pitcher Maud Nelson, who joined the club in 1897. The sixteen-year-old pitching sensation led the team to a string of victories as they traveled across the country; local newspapers described her as "phenomenal" with excellent speed and an extensive repertoire of pitches. Of the team as a whole, the Eugene, Oregon *Guard* stated that, "the girls from Beantown put up a clean game and play like professionals, asking for no favors, but playing a hard snappy game on its merits." Nelson eventually left the team to organize her own barnstorming outfit, but returned to the Boston Bloomer Girls in 1917, and was still pitching for them five years later at age 41. The edition of the team shown in this photograph, from after the turn of the century, includes at least two men. It was common practice in those days to include several male players on Bloomer Girl teams, sometimes disguising them with wigs and rouge. *Photo courtesy of Michael Olenick.*

Smokey Joe Wood, one of the fastest pitchers in baseball history, shortly after joining the Boston Red Sox. Wood made his major-league debut in 1908 at the age of 18. His professional career had begun two years earlier when he was paid $20 to play for a Bloomer Girls barnstorming team; Wood later recalled the team manager telling him that he had such a baby face that he wouldn't need to bother putting on a wig or makeup to pass for female. In 1912, Wood had perhaps the finest season any pitcher ever enjoyed, posting a 34-5 record with 10 shutouts; that year, renowned fireballer Walter Johnson told an interviewer, "Can I throw harder than Joe Wood? Listen, my friend, there's no man alive can throw harder than Smokey Joe Wood." When his arm burned out, Wood continued as an outfielder for another five years, and once led his team in batting with a .366 average. He later became baseball coach at Yale, serving in that capacity for twenty years. *Photo courtesy of Bob Wood.*

Sept. 8, 1909: Champs Took Liberties With His Benders

Although Worcester's last appearance in the major leagues was in 1882, the city continued to field powerful teams in the Eastern League and the New England League. In 1909, as a member of the latter association, Worcester was managed by Jesse Burkett, a future Hall-of-Famer who twice batted over .400 in the majors. The team had won three straight championships from 1906 to 1908, earning the simple nickname "Champs." As Burkett's club pursued another pennant, the *Worcester Gazette* reported on a critical late-season game:

BURKETT'S MEN TAKE ONE FROM DOWD'S WHALERS
Bauman's Costly Errors and Champs Timely Hitting Turn Trick.

The Champs walloped New Bedford 8 to 1 yesterday, and did it just as easily as the score would indicate once they struck their gait. It was a close game of ball, although neither team displayed much ginger for five innings. The Champs found Syfert in the sixth and took liberties with his benders during the rest of the game. Beauman [sic], the visitors' shortstop, gave an exhibition of weird throwing in the fifth inning that was the limit. He heaved two high and wide to first and did a subway stunt on a throw to the plate.

Andy Owens pitched a good game for the Champs, but the Whalers got to him in the sixth and eighth innings, good support and some bad work on the bases helping Owens out. Logan and Yerkes were a stone wall on the defense, while Bradley put up his usual classy game at first.

The score:—

WORCESTER

	ab.	r.	1b.	po.	a.	e.
Shaw, 3b	4	1	1	0	1	0
Yerkes, ss	4	1	0	3	5	0
Bradley, 1b	3	0	1	16	0	0
Rondeau, rf	5	1	1	2	1	0
Logan, 2b	4	0	2	2	5	0
Russell, lf	3	1	1	2	0	0
Kiernan, cf	4	3	2	0	0	2
McCune, c	2	1	2	2	2	0
Owens, p	4	0	0	0	4	0
Totals	33	8	10	27	18	2

NEW BEDFORD

	ab.	r.	1b.	po.	a.	e.
Barrows, lf	3	1	2	5	0	0
Keller, 1b	3	0	1	6	1	0
Cunningham, 2b	3	0	1	4	2	1
Bauman, ss	4	0	0	2	2	4
Wilson, 3b	4	0	1	1	1	0
Crum, cf	3	0	0	3	0	0
Griffith, rf	3	0	0	0	0	0
O'Leary, c	3	0	0	2	2	0
Syfert, p	3	0	0	1	4	0
Totals	29	1	5	24	12	5

Innings	1	2	3	4	5	6	7	8	9		
Worcester	0	0	0	0	1	3	2	2	-	—	8
New Bedford	0	0	0	0	0	1	0	0	0	—	1

Two-base hits—Barrows, Cunningham, Keller, Shaw, Kiernan. Sacrifice hits—McCune 2, Bradley, Crum, Keller. Stolen bases—McCune, Kiernan, Wilson. Left on bases—Worcester 7; New Bedford 5. First base on balls—Off Owens 1, off Syfert 3. First base on errors—Worcester 4, New Bedford 1. Struck out—By Owens 1, by Syfert 1. Wild pitches—Syfert 2. Time—1h. 45m. Umpire—Connolly.

Three days after "walloping" New Bedford, Worcester defeated Haverhill to win its fourth consecutive New England League pennant.

Sadder than the team's mediocre showing was the fact that Cy Young had made his final appearance in a Red Sox uniform. The 41-year-old Young won 21 games for Boston, including a June 30 no-hitter (the third in his career) against New York in Hilltop Park. It was the fifteenth and last time that he would win 20 games in a season. He would pitch only three more years before retiring.

On April 16, 1909, Harry Hooper made his big-league debut with the Red Sox. Hooper was an engineer who agreed to play baseball for Boston in part because he was interested in the new ballpark that the team was planning to build. As one of the best outfielders in the game, he stayed in the major leagues for seventeen years—eleven of them with Boston—and was later elected to the Hall of Fame.

Although Hooper was an important addition to the starting line-up, the pitching staff couldn't recover from the loss of Cy Young. Boston's top three pitchers in 1909 were Frank Arellanes (who had won 4 games for the Red Sox in his rookie season of 1908), Eddie Cicotte, and Smokey Joe Wood, who posted 16, 13, and 11 wins, respectively.

Still under the direction of manager Fred Lake, the club wound up with a third-place finish in 1909. Soon, however, the Boston Red Sox would win four World Championships in a span of seven years.

6

1910–1918:
Miracle Braves and World Champion Red Sox

As the twentieth century entered its second decade, professional baseball was enjoying unprecedented prosperity. Attendance at major-league games nearly doubled over the period from 1903 to 1910. Minor-league baseball was thriving as well; there were approximately forty minor leagues in 1910, attracting more than twenty million fans a year.

With ticket sales booming, stylish new parks, constructed of steel and concrete instead of wood, were built to accommodate the fans. In the six years from 1909 to 1915, baseball's all-time jewel boxes were dedicated: Fenway Park and Braves Field in Boston, Wrigley Field and Comiskey Park in Chicago, Brooklyn's Ebbets Field, Detroit's Tiger Stadium, Pittsburgh's Forbes Field, Crosley Field in Cincinnati, League Park in Cleveland, Griffith Stadium in Washington DC, and the rebuilt Polo Grounds in New York. The new parks included dressing rooms for visiting teams (who prior to this had to change at their hotels), concession stands for hungry fans, and roofs on the dugouts to protect players from projectiles.

The game was even gaining international attention. The 1911 World Series was in fact followed worldwide, with trans-Pacific cable carrying game results to Tokyo and other Asian cities. In the winter of 1913–14, the New York Giants and Chicago White Sox embarked on a world tour, playing in Japan, the Philippines, Australia, Egypt, France, and England. Nearer to home, major leaguers played numerous exhibition and spring training games in Cuba, Mexico, and Central and South America.

Since the truce of 1903 between the American and National Leagues, organized baseball was governed by the National Commission, which consisted of the presidents of both major leagues and a chairman elected by the owners. In effect, the game was run by American League president Ban Johnson. National League leadership was inconsistent (from 1902 to 1913, the National League had five different presidents), and Commission chairman August "Garry" Herrmann, although president of the National League Cincinnati Reds, was an old friend of Johnson's and usually sided with the American Leaguer.

Above: Pitcher "Happy Jack" Chesbro, a former mental hospital attendant from North Adams, Massachusetts set a twentieth century record by winning 41 games for the New York Highlanders (Yankees) in 1904. A wild pitch he threw on the final day of that season, however, gave Boston the pennant. Chesbro's last major-league appearance came five years later, with the 1909 Boston Red Sox. After posting a 0–5 record, he retired to become baseball coach of Amherst College. He also continued to played semi-pro ball, and in 1910 he finally won a championship, pitching the Whitinsville, Massachusetts team shown here to a mill league title. *Below:* A 1911 game in Boston's Huntington Avenue Grounds. Note the sign on the fence advertising "Nuf Ced" McGreevey's Third Base Saloon: "How can You get Home without Reaching 3rd Base? Nuf Ced." The building to the right is the Boston Opera House. *Photo courtesy of Michael Gershman.*

The structure of major league baseball remained unchallenged until 1914, when a third league tried to get in on the baseball "boom." The Federal League had operated as an independent league in the Midwest in 1913, using semi-pro players, former major-leaguers, and some minor-league second stringers. The next season, the Feds followed the example that Ban Johnson had set a dozen years earlier: franchises were established in Eastern cities, the established leagues were raided for star players, and the Federal League declared itself to be a third major league. War ensued for two years, until the Federal League folded at the end of the 1915 season. After the demise of the Federal League, the franchises that comprised major-league baseball would remain unchanged for nearly four decades—until 1953, when the Boston Braves relocated to Milwaukee.

By 1910, the playing rules had evolved almost to the point where they are today. The most important change during the decade was to the ball itself: in 1911, for the first time, the regulation baseball had a cork center. With this livelier ball, National League home runs went up almost fifty percent and the American League batting average jumped thirty points (there would be an even greater power explosion in the next decade). There was some new equipment as well: shin guards, which had been introduced for catchers in 1907, became a standard part of their gear, and the first known protective cup, made of solid steel, was worn in 1916.

Among the players who broke into the major leagues during the decade were pitchers Grover Cleveland Alexander, Burleigh Grimes, and Babe Ruth; infielders Rogers Hornsby, Rabbit Maranville, and George Sisler; outfielders Harry Heilmann, Edd Roush, and Casey Stengel. These stars would go on to bridge the dead ball and lively eras.

The good times for baseball were soon to suffer a reversal, however. By the end of the decade, war and scandal would take a severe toll on the game. When America entered World War I in 1917, baseball owners attempted to obtain an exemption for ballplayers—a move that didn't sit well with much of the patriotic public. Attendance figures plummeted, and shortened seasons were played in 1918 and 1919. Worse was to come the following year, when members of the Chicago White Sox were found to have conspired with gamblers to throw the 1919 World Series.

It would take years for the game to recover, and by then baseball was in a new era, dominated by *former* Red Sox star Babe Ruth.

TWIN STATE LEAGUE

The Twin State League came about largely because there was going to be a ballpark built with no one to play in it. Brattleboro, Vermont businessmen George Fox and Michael Moran planned to build an amusement park on the nearby island in the Connecticut River. Island Park, as they dubbed it, would have a ballroom, bowling alleys, and a shooting arcade; there would be concerts, dances, movies, and vaudeville shows. And, there would be a new baseball park, with a 1,200 seat grandstand, built adjacent to the amusement pavilion.

Excited at the promise of Island Park, Brattleboro baseball fans undertook a subscription drive that raised $1,000 for a team to play in the facility. Of course, a team needed opponents, so the next goal was to organize a league. With the participation of a couple more Connecticut River Valley towns—Bellows Falls, Vermont, and Keene, New Hampshire—the Twin State Baseball League was founded on March 12, 1911. The new league was part of Organized Baseball, with Class "D" status. In its inaugural season, four teams played a 36-game schedule: Bellows Falls Sulphites, Brattleboro Islanders, Keene Champs, and a team that was literally "twin state": the Hyphens, representing Springfield, Vermont, and Charlestown, New Hampshire. For all four franchises, it was the first time that these towns had fielded professional baseball nines.

Opening Day for the new league was July 1, with new Island Park the site of the first contest. Before the game, the Islanders and the visiting Bellows Falls squad met at Brattleboro Town Hall; they then paraded down Main Street and across the road bridge to Island Park, with the town's First Regiment Band leading the procession. A full crowd was on hand to watch as Brattleboro took a 8–3 win over the Sulphites.

The Islanders were managed by E. L. "Home Run" Breckinridge, who had earned his nickname by hitting 120 homers in the minor leagues, which was a remarkable total in the dead ball era (Frank "Home Run" Baker only totaled 96 four-baggers in his major-league career). Breckinridge was a respected baseball man with a long history in the region; after twelve seasons as a player, he had umpired in the New England League and coached baseball at Amherst, Dartmouth, and Williams colleges.

Three weeks into the season, Brattleboro lost Charles Ivers, its captain and best hitter, to a broken leg. Under Breckinridge's guidance, however, the Islanders continued to battle the Keene Champs for first place in the standings.

On the final day of the season, in what the Vermont *Phoenix* called "the game of a lifetime," the Brattleboro Islanders defeated Keene 2–0 in Island Park to win the league's first championship.

The 1911 Twin State League also marked what is probably the first appearance of an African-American player in twentieth century organized baseball. Catcher Bill Thompson, a veteran of black barnstorming clubs (according to the *Brattleboro Reformer,* he was "formerly of the Cuban Giants and the best independent teams of New England"), played most of 1911 for the Bellows Falls Sulphites, until he suffered a season-ending hand injury. He was among the league's top batsmen, hitting .288 in a season when the league leader won the batting title with a .300 average. Thompson was respected for his talents and there are no known reports of racial incidents. The *Bellows Falls Times* said of his catching abilities, "Bill Thompson's mit [sic] nails everything behind the plate and his throwing is the real thing." When the *Cheshire Republican* of Springfield, Vermont, held a reader's poll, Thompson was voted the best catcher in the league. After his injury forced him off the roster, Thompson was given a front page tribute in the *Bellows Falls Times*, which reported, "Bill Thompson, the hero of many a good game this summer, is resting at Concord, New Hampshire. Bill was sure fast company and his headwork behind the plate and stickwork at all times was a great factor in the local victories of the season. If Bill's fingers were OK there would be no hiking for Concord when he did. His departure met with the sincere regret of all good ball lovers, not only here but in the other towns of the league."

Sept. 4, 1911: The Islanders Are Now The Champs

Since the construction of Island Park helped bring about the birth of the Twin State League, it is fitting that the League's first championship was decided in the park. The September 4, 1911 game between Brattleboro and Keene attracted more than 3,200 fans from all parts of Southern Vermont and New Hampshire. According to the *Vermont Phoenix*, "More than 500 Keene supporters came to see the game in automobiles and on a special train and Bellows Falls sent a delegation of more than 200. The large crowd was handled without a hitch, there was not the semblance of rowdyism on anybody's part and it was a fitting climax to a two months' race for the leadership of the league." Keene was shutout 2–0 by the Islanders and the *Brattleboro Reformer* hailed the victory:

TWIN STATE LEAGUE CHAMPIONSHIP IS OURS
Brattleboro Team Won Pennant Monday When It
Defeated Keene in Final Contest of the Series.

OVER 3,200 PEOPLE WITNESSED DECIDING GAME
Which Was a Pitchers' Battle Between Bosk and Smith, Former Having a
Slight Advantage—Close of a Highly Successful Season Brought Out Largest
Crowd Ever at a Ball Game in Southern Vermont—
Management Deserves Commendation.

The Twin State league pennant belongs to Brattleboro, and will float at the head of the tall staff at Island park until another baseball season rolls by. The Islanders are now the Champs and will be known by that title until some other team gains the right to adopt it. The matter was settled Monday afternoon when in the final game of the league race Brattleboro defeated Keene 2 to 0, thereby finishing two games ahead of its New Hampshire rival.

The score:

BRATTLEBORO

	ab	r	h	po	a	e
Nichols, 2b	2	0	0	1	2	0
Vance, ss	4	1	1	2	4	0
Horan, 3b	4	0	1	3	4	0
Murray, 1b	4	0	0	10	2	0
Wachtel, lf	3	0	0	2	0	1
McLeod, rf	3	0	1	0	0	0
Edgar, cf	3	1	0	1	0	0
Bosk, p	3	0	1	3	1	0
Ensign, c	2	0	0	5	0	0
Totals	28	2	4	27	13	1

KEENE

	ab	r	h	po	a	e
Durgin, rf	4	0	0	2	0	0
Leonard, 1b	4	0	0	8	0	1
Finnegan, ss	4	0	1	0	2	0
McCrehan, lf	4	0	2	0	0	0
Donovan, 2b	3	0	0	1	0	0
McCarthy, cf	3	0	0	4	0	0
Qualters, 3b	3	0	0	0	3	0
Delaney, c	3	0	0	9	0	0
Smith, p	3	0	0	0	1	0
Totals	31	0	3	24	6	1

Innings	1	2	3	4	5	6	7	8	9		
Brattleboro	1	0	0	0	0	0	1	0	x	—	2

(Box score note: it was common practice not to list an inning-by-inning score for a team that was shut out.)

Sacrifice hits, Donovan, Edgar. First base on balls, off Bosk 1, off Smith 1. Left on bases, Brattleboro 5, Keene 5. Struck out, by Smith 10, by Bosk 4. Batter hit, Nichols 2. Wild pitch, Bosk. Time, 1h, 38m. Umpires, Finn and Shea.

Two years later, when Bellows Falls signed a black pitcher name Wickware, the other clubs of the league voted to ban any players "other than white men." Bellows Falls was the only team to vote against the ban.

After the 1911 season, the Twin State League was no longer part of Organized Baseball, but continued as an independent ("outlaw") league. The Springfield-Charlestown Hyphens disbanded, and were replaced by the Northampton Larks who went on to win the 1912 pennant in an expanded 48-game season.

In 1913, the league increased to six teams, adding franchises in Newport, New Hampshire, and Greenfield, Massachusetts. Briefly appearing for Brattleboro during the 1913 season was pitcher Doc Crandall, who was in the middle of a ten-year career in the major leagues. Crandall played eleven games for the Vermont team to stay in shape while under suspension by New York Giants manager John McGraw. The Crandall case is but one example of the numerous interactions between the Twin State League and big league clubs. Because the Twin State League operated outside the bounds of Organized Baseball, transactions were casual. A major-league club (usually from Boston or New York) might "borrow" a Twin State player for a game or two to fill in for an injured regular; or, a big-leaguer like Crandall might bolster the roster of one of the Twin State teams for a while.

After an exciting 1913 pennant race in which only three games separated the top five teams in the final standings, the league elected to play a longer, 60-game schedule the following year. All of the teams made it through the 1914 season, and Newport edged out Keene for the pennant. The three poorest teams—Brattleboro, Greenfield, and Northampton—were unable to go on for another season, however, and folded operations.

Claremont, New Hampshire, was added in 1915 to bring the league back up to four teams. Newport again took the title in what would be the league's final season. Attendance at Keene games was so low that the team would only play road games in the final month of the season. This presented a problem since Keene was the only franchise left in the league after September 7. The Twin State League folded and professional baseball in Vermont wasn't re-established until 1923.

June 8, 1912: Old Rivals Fight Hard

Harvard's longest standing baseball rivalry is not with Yale, but with Brown University. On June 27, 1863, the Harvard '66 Base Ball Club traveled to the Dexter Training Ground in Providence to play the Brown Class of '65 team in the first intercollegiate game for both schools. Harvard took that contest by a score of 27–17, and completed dominated Brown for the next fifteen years (in the 1870–71 season, the colleges played each other three times, Harvard winning by scores of 55–24, 42–10, and 34–15). Brown did not win a game against the Crimson until May 3, 1879, when J. Lee Richmond launched his phenomenal 1879 season by pitching Brown to a 21–5 victory over the Cambridge school. By the turn of the century, the school nines were of comparable strength, and the rivalry intensified. Interest was high enough that matches between the two universities attracted crowds that would be considered good-sized for major-league ballparks. On June 8, 1912, Brown defeated Harvard for the second time of the season before 5,000 fans in Providence. The *Providence Journal* reported on the latest match between the "old rivals:"

BROWN CONQUERS HARVARD, 2 TO 1
Old Rivals Fight Hard for Decision on Andrews Field

5000 SEE THE CONTEST
Warner Pitches Hill Men to Victory.
Crimson Starts Hardy, Who Lasts Less Than an Inning, Retiring in Favor of Bartholf, Who is Hit Freely.

A smoking three-bagger by Durgin gave Brown a victory in the second battle with the Harvard nine yesterday afternoon on Andrews field, the final score standing 2 to 1.

The Brown bear did not have anything particular to be proud of, however, in his kill. There were comparatively few brilliant spots in the whole nine innings and what there were were practically divided between the teams.

Warner, the Brown southpaw, did not pitch his usual steady game, although he only passed four men and struck out six. The Harvard slant men, however, had even harder going, Hardy lasting but two-thirds of the first inning when, after he had passed three men and filled the bases with two down, "Doc" Sexton yanked him out and sent Bartholf to the mound. He managed to finish the game and only passed one man, although he was touched up freely.

From the very start of the contest it was easy to see that both teams were on their toes and were keyed up with excitement. Both were out to get the long end of the decision and this probably was accountable for some of the loose playing.

One of the largest crowds of the season turned out for the game, fully 5000 people filling the big stands.

> *Contrary to the usual custom, two umpires were used, Bedford holding the indicator on balls and strikes throughout the game, while O'Rourke looked after the bases. The work of the latter was excellent, two or three of the decisions on the bases calling for extremely quick work, but the former's decisions did not always meet with approval.*
>
> *The score:*

BROWN	ab	1b	po	a	e		HARVARD	ab	1b	po	a	e
Crowther, r	3	1	1	0	0		Wingate, s	2	1	1	2	0
Dukette, 2	2	0	0	0	0		Bolton, m	4	0	4	0	0
K. Nash, s	3	0	1	3	1		Potter, 2	4	1	2	2	0
Snell, c	4	0	5	1	0		Clark, 1	4	0	9	1	0
Loud, l	3	1	1	0	0		Babson, l	4	1	1	0	0
Durgin, 1	4	2	12	1	0		Gibson, 3	4	0	0	2	0
Reilly, 3	4	2	1	2	0		Wiggles'h, r	3	0	1	0	0
R. Nash, m	2	1	5	1	0		Young, c	4	0	6	0	0
Warner, p	2	0	0	3	1		Hardy, p	0	0	0	1	1
							Bartholf, p	1	0	0	3	0
Totals	27	7	26*	11	2		Totals	30	3	24	11	1

* Babson out on third strike foul bunt.

Innings	1	2	3	4	5	6	7	8	9		
Brown	0	1	0	0	0	0	0	1		—	2
Harvard	0	0	0	0	1	0	0	0	0	—	1

> *Runs—Loud, Reilly—2; Wingate—1. Stolen bases—K. Nash, Durgin, Loud, Bolton. Two-base hit—Babson. Three-base hit—Durgin. Sacrifice hits—Dukette, Warner. Sacrifice fly—Dukette. Struck out—By Warner 5; by Hardy 1; by Bartholf 4. First base on balls—Off Warner 4; off Hardy 3; off Bartholf 1. Wild pitch—Bartholf. Hit by pitched ball—By Warner—Wingate. Left on bases—Brown 8, Harvard 7. Umpires—Bedford and O'Rourke. Time—1 h. 50m. Attendance—5,000.*

FENWAY PARK

Each year from 1909 to 1911, the Boston Red Sox dropped a notch lower in the final standings, finishing in third, fourth, and fifth places. Team president John I. Taylor tired of his baseball hobby, and decided to sell the team—but first he wanted to increase its value.

Taylor owned the franchise and the Huntington Avenue Grounds, but he did not own the land on which the park was built (he leased the site from the New York, New Haven, and Hartford Railroad). To make the sale of the Red Sox a more profitable package deal, he decided to build a new ballpark in another location. He chose the Fenway section of Boston, an undeveloped area of filled-in marshland (fens). Taylor was part owner of the Fenway Realty Company, so he simply sold himself some cheap

This photograph taken during the September 4, 1911 game that decided the Twin State League championship shows the fans packed around the playing field of Island Park. The grandstand could hold 1,200 people, but nearly three times that number showed up for the game, making it the largest crowd ever to witness a baseball game in southern Vermont. Behind the fans and trees can be seen the Connecticut River. *Photo courtesy of Brattleboro Photos, Inc.*

land near Lansdowne Street, and began plans to build a baseball park. Ground was broken for Fenway Park in September, 1911. Three months later, with construction barely under way, Taylor's investment paid off when he sold the club—land included—for a hefty $150,000.

The new Red Sox owners were Jimmy McAleer, Bob McRoy, and Jake Stahl. McAleer, who had been in baseball for almost thirty years as a player and manager, was named president, and McRoy served as treasurer. American League president Ban Johnson had an active role behind the scenes and was believed to have been a secret investor. He had close ties to both McAleer and McRoy: McAleer had helped Johnson recruit National League players in the junior league's early days, and McRoy had served as Johnson's secretary. Jake Stahl, who had retired after the 1910 season to take a job in banking, did triple duty for the Red Sox in 1912: part-owner, manager, and first baseman.

The days leading up to the first game in Fenway Park weren't promising ones: construction hadn't been completed, the public's attention had been diverted by the sinking of the *Titanic* two days before the scheduled opener, and steady rains postponed the inaugural contest by three days. Finally, on April 20, although the park had not yet been dedicated and there was still some construction work to be done, 27,000 fans filled the new ballpark to see the Red Sox host the visiting New York Highlanders (soon to be renamed the "Yankees"). The Boston rooters were treated to an extra-inning 7-6 victory over the New Yorkers, with the winning run driven in by Tris Speaker in the eleventh inning.

From then on, Boston continued to pile up victories, never dropping lower than second in the standings. By early June, the Red Sox were in first place to stay.

The Boston outfield of 1912 is still considered by many to be the best outfield (especially defensively) in baseball history. In addition to Tris Speaker in center field and Harry Hooper in right, Duffy Lewis (who would later earn the distinction of being the first player to pinch hit for Babe Ruth) patrolled left field. Lewis was an agile outfielder who'd made his debut with the Red Sox in 1910. In Fenway Park, which featured a tricky incline in left field, Lewis became so adept at fielding balls off the embankment that the area became known as "Duffy's Cliff." The "Golden Outfield" of Lewis, Speaker, and Hooper remained together for six years, from 1910 through 1915.

The infielders were overshadowed by their counterparts in the outfield, but they played solid baseball throughout the season. As a first baseman, Jake Stahl's return from retirement was a success: he played in most of the team's games and batted over .300 for the first time in his career. Third baseman Larry Gardner hit a career-high .315. The club was weakest in its keystone combination of Heinie Wagner at shortstop and Steve Yerkes (in his second season with the Sox) at second, but these players, too, made contributions to keep the team winning.

The undisputed star of the pitching staff was Smokey Joe Wood. Wood had won 23 games in 1911, including a no-hitter over the St. Louis Browns. In 1912, he surpassed this record, enjoying one of the most spectacular seasons in baseball history. Relying on a blazing fastball, the twenty-two-year-old posted a record of 34 wins against only 5 defeats, with 10 shutouts, 258 strikeouts, and an earned run average of 1.91.

Although eclipsed by Joe Wood, the other Red Sox pitchers also turned in fine seasons. Rookie Hugh Bedient won 20 games while losing nine. Buck O'Brien, a native of Brockton, Massachusetts, was also a 20-game winner in his first full season with the Sox. Charley "Sea Lion" Hall won a career-high 15 games, and Ray Collins, a Northern League veteran from Colchester, Vermont, contributed 13 victories.

Handling the pitching staff was Bill "Rough" Carrigan, who led the league's catchers in fielding. Carrigan also directed much of the action on the field, and would soon become the Red Sox manager.

The Washington Senators provided Boston with some competition for the title, but as the Red Sox pulled away from the rest of the league, the only real competition left was an individual one between the Senators' Walter Johnson and Boston's Smokey Joe Wood. Early in the season, Johnson had set an American League record by winning 16 games in a row (on his way to a total of 33). Then Joe Wood put together a string of victories to challenge Johnson's new record. On September 6, with Wood's streak standing at 13, the two great pitchers faced each other in Fenway Park. Interest was so high that the Red Sox sold dugout space as well as part of the outfield to the overflow crowd (the players had to sit in chairs along the foul lines). In a thrilling duel, Wood kept his streak alive with a 1–0 win over Johnson. The winning run scored when Tris Speaker knocked a ground-rule double into the swarm of fans on the outfield grass and Duffy Lewis followed with another double to drive him home.

At the end of the season, the Red Sox had set an American League record by winning 105 games. Tris Speaker was named the league's Most Valuable Player by the

The "Golden Outfield" that played together for the Red Sox from 1910 to 1915: right fielder Harry Hooper, centerfielder Tris Speaker, and left fielder Duffy Lewis. Many baseball historians still consider this trio to be the best fielding outfield of all time.

baseball writers; "The Grey Eagle" batted .383, led the league in doubles with 53, tied for the lead in homers with 10, and stole 52 bases.

Boston then prepared to play John McGraw's New York Giants in the World Series (McGraw couldn't get out of it this year, as he had in 1904). It turned out to be one of the most exciting series ever—and not only because of what happened between the foul lines.

The opener was played in New York, with Joe Wood earning a 4–3 victory. The next day, the teams were in Boston for the second game; after 11 innings, the score stood 6–6 when darkness put an end to the contest and it was ruled a tie. New York evened the series the next day when Rube Marquard outdueled Buck O'Brien 2–1. Boston took the next two games on wins by Wood and Hugh Bedient, for a three games to one advantage.

Then the trouble started. Jake Stahl had Smokey Joe Wood slated to pitch the sixth game in New York. Wood wanted to pitch, and the Boston players wanted their ace to take the mound and close out the series. But Jimmy McAleer had other ideas. As team president, he ordered Stahl to start Buck O'Brien instead and keep Wood in reserve for a Game Seven in case O'Brien lost (baseball writer Fred Lieb suggested that McAleer might have been half-hoping that the series would have to go back to Boston so he could collect another game's gate receipts). This caused a bitter rift between McAleer and Stahl that never healed. The Red Sox players were angry with the front-office interference, and O'Brien was thrown off his game by having to pitch when he knew

Boston police doing battle with the Royal Rooters in Fenway Park before the seventh game of the 1912 World Series. In a front office blunder, Red Sox management had sold off the pavilion seats traditionally reserved for the Rooters. Led by Mayor John "Honey Fitz" Fitzgerald, 500 Royal Rooters charged onto the playing field and took up a position on Duffy's Cliff. The angry fan club successfully fought off the foot patrolmen who attempted to remove them. Mounted police were called in as reinforcements and finally drove the mayor of Boston and the rest of the Royal Rooters from the field. The New York Giants went on to win, forcing an eighth game to decide the series (Game Two had ended in a tie). Boston fans were outraged at the treatment of Fitzgerald and the Royal Rooters, and public apologies from Red Sox executives failed to placate them. On the following day, Fenway Park was half-empty as the Red Sox beat New York 3–2 in ten innings to win the World Series. *Photo Courtesy of the Boston Public Library, Print Department.*

his teammates wanted someone else on the mound. O'Brien was knocked from the box after giving up five runs in the first inning, and the Giants pulled to within a game of tying the series.

Another front office blunder occurred before Game Seven in Fenway Park, when the club sold the seats that had traditionally been reserved for the Royal Rooters. Just before Joe Wood was to throw the opening pitch of the game, five hundred members of the booster club, led by Boston mayor John "Honey Fitz" Fitzgerald, stormed the field and took positions on Duffy's Cliff. By the time police drove the Rooters off the field, Wood's arm was cold. Like O'Brien the day before, Wood lasted only one inning, giving up six runs. New York tied the series with a 11–4 win.

The final game (number eight, because of the tie in Game Two) was also played in Fenway Park, as determined by a coin flip. Although the previous games had all drawn more than 30,000 fans, only 17,000 were on hand for the finale. Angry at the way the beloved Royal Rooters had been treated by the club, fans stayed away from what would a remarkable conclusion to the World Series. Christy Mathewson and Hugh Bedient were pitching a 1–1 tie into the eighth inning when Smokey Joe Wood was

Sept. 14, 1912: The Catching of Ancient Jim O'Rourke

Hall-of-Famer Jim O'Rourke of Bridgeport, Connecticut, made his professional debut in 1872 as a shortstop with the Middletown Mansfields of the National Association. After eighteen years in the major leagues, he returned to his home town to manage the Bridgeport entry in the Connecticut League. O'Rourke served as the team's manager from 1897 to 1908, and as president of the league from 1907 to 1913 (in his role as president he once fined himself for using profanity while performing his managerial duties). Forty years after his debut, O'Rourke played his final game in organized baseball, at age 62, in a game between the first-place New Haven Wings and the last-place Waterbury Spuds. Although he apparently had difficulty donning the catcher's gear, he played a fine game according to the *New Haven Union*:

WINGS AND SPUDS SPLIT DOUBLE BILL
JIM O'ROURKE IN LOCAL UNIFORM CATCHES THE FIRST GAME

Two slug-fests terminated the state league season on the Savin Rock baseball grounds yesterday afternoon and when the double bill was brought to a close it was found that honors for the day had been divided by the New Haven and Waterbury teams. Murphy's Spuds took the first number, 10 to 4, while Connell's pennant possessors in the second game routed the Brass City bunch by a tally of 13 to 3. Despite the heavy scoring and hitting the double-header was played in almost record time—both games, including the 5-minute intermission, taking but a little over three hours to play. Both contests were of course one-sided and the victories were never in doubt, nevertheless the afternoon was illuminated by several features that made the 1,200 fans present satisfied as they began their hikes for home.

In the first place, President James H. O'Rourke of the Connecticut league, aged 61 years [actually 62] and the dean of all baseball players, caught the entire first game for the New Haven team and his fielding game, although it was the first he played this year, would have been the envy of many another catcher in this circuit. He skipped about the diamond like a yearling and his activity put about 15 of the other players on the same field to shame.

The real feature of this contest was the catching of ancient Jim O'Rourke. Twice on fielders' choice, he reached first and twice died on hard infield slams. He held up the erratic Foster in first class style and the applause which greeted him as he donned the mask, mit and windpad, will be remembered by the great old veteran for years to come. Nagle of New Haven acted as Jim's waist valet during his session in the game and at the opening some job was on Jack's hands when he attempted to buckle a brand-new windpad around the massive form of O'Rourke.

Miller's home run and O'Rourke's back-stoping [sic] were the only bright lights in the locals' play.

(First Game):

WATERBURY	ab.	r.	h.	po.	a.	e.
Eley, lf	5	2	3	4	0	0
Nichols, cf	5	2	2	2	1	0
Hoey, rf	5	1	1	1	0	0
Cabrera, ss	5	1	1	1	7	0
Warner, 2b	5	1	2	6	2	0
Gygil, 1b	4	1	2	10	2	1
Lemieux, 3b	4	1	2	0	3	0
Brennan, c	5	1	1	3	0	0
Lower, p	4	0	1	0	2	0
Totals	42	10	15	27	17	1

NEW HAVEN	ab.	r.	h.	po.	a.	e.
Pepe, ss	6	0	3	1	3	0
Flick, 2b	5	0	2	3	5	0
Gough, cf	5	1	1	3	0	1
Foster, rf	5	0	0	1	0	0
Miller, 1b	4	3	2	12	0	1
Sherwood, 3b	3	0	2	2	2	0
Daschbach, lf	3	0	0	1	0	0
O'Rourke, c	4	0	0	4	1	0
E. Foster, p	4	0	0	0	3	0
Totals	39	4	10	27	14	2

Innings	1	2	3	4	5	6	7	8	9		
Waterbury	2	0	0	0	0	8	0	0	0	—	10
Brattleboro	0	1	0	1	0	0	0	1	1	—	4

Home runs, Miller and Cabrera; two base hits, Miller, Flick; stolen base, Gygli; sacrifice hits, Hoey 2; double plays, Lemieux, Warner and Gygli; Cabrera, Warner and Gygli; Flick and Miller; left on bases, New Haven 10, Waterbury 6; struck out, by Foster 3, by Lower 1; bases on balls, off Foster 1, off Lower 5; hit by pitched ball, Foster 1; umpire, Held; time, 1:25.

In the final week of the season, New Haven had a large enough lead in the standings that the White Wings were assured of winning the league championship. What was unclear was whether any of them would end up in jail. A local politician tried to have the entire team arrested for playing games on Sundays in violation of an ordinance against Sunday ball playing. New Haven City Attorney John Booth was unable to issue arrest warrants, however, when he could find no witnesses willing to identify the players involved—despite the fact that there were typically 2,000 fans in attendance at these games.

brought in to relieve Bedient. The deadlock continued into the tenth, when Wood gave up a run to the Giants in the top of the inning. Down to their last three outs, the Red Sox rallied—with the help of some New York miscues. Giants center fielder Fred Snodgrass dropped an easy fly ball to put the leadoff batter on second base. Mathewson then walked weak-hitting Steve Yerkes. Tris Speaker followed by lifting a foul pop-up near first base, which three Giants watched fall to the ground; given a reprieve, Speaker promptly smacked a double that tied the game and put the winning run on third base. Larry Gardner drove the run home with a long fly to right field, giving the Boston Red Sox their first World Championship in their new ballpark.

But the trouble that had begun in the latter part of the series continued. Jimmy McAleer fired Jake Stahl midway through the next season. Public outrage at the club's officials continued, and McAleer and Bob McRoy sold their interest in the team one year after winning the championship. The turmoil had its effect on the team's play: the World Champions finished the 1913 season in fifth place, more than thirty games behind the new pennant winners.

MIRACLE BRAVES

The Boston Braves of 1914 didn't literally "come from nowhere"—but they'd certainly been loitering in the vicinity of nowhere long enough to have established squatters' rights. In the four years from 1909 through 1912, the team finished in last place every season, losing 108, 100, 107, and 101 games.

Serious efforts to turn things around finally started to be made in 1913. James E. Gaffney, a contractor and politician connected to New York's infamous Tammany Hall, acquired controlling interest in the club. Gaffney promptly adopted the Tammany Hall symbol, Indian Chief Tamenund, as the team's logo and changed the club's name to the "Braves" (Boston thus had a baseball team named for a corrupt New York political machine).

One of Gaffney's first moves was to hire George Tweedy Stallings to manage the team. Stallings had a playing career that consisted of seven games, and just over four years of managerial experience with three different teams. Off the field, Stallings (who was the son of a Confederate general) had the manner of a soft-spoken Southern gentleman. Once a game was in progress, however, he turned into a hot-tempered tyrant who cursed his own players, opponents, and umpires. Boston's new manager was also one of the most superstitious men in baseball history; wearing a suit and bow tie, he patrolled the ground in front of the dugout during games, picking up any nearby scraps of paper, which he considered bad luck (once opposing teams found out about this particular quirk, they made sure that there would always be plenty of litter in front of the Braves dugout to keep Stallings agitated).

There were some other additions to the 1913 Boston team that would prove to be key elements a year later. Diminutive pitcher Dick "The Bald Eagle" Rudolph came to Boston from the New York Giants, where he had posted a record of 0–1 in two seasons. Rudolph had a great curve, pinpoint control, and perhaps the least effective spitball in baseball history (his own catcher, Hank Gowdy, would later say, "As for Dick's spitter, about the best you could say for it was that it was wet."). Strong-armed rookie Bill James was also added to the pitching staff. Rudolph and James joined veteran hurlers Lefty Tyler, from Derry, New Hampshire and Hub Perdue, who had led the Braves in wins in 1912 with 13.

1913 marked the first full season for future Hall-of-Famer Rabbit Maranville, a sure-fielding pixieish shortstop. Over the course of a 23-year big league career, playing in 2,670 games, Maranville often led National League shortstops in fielding categories, and usually led both leagues in practical jokes.

Under their new manager, the Braves improved to a fifth-place finish in 1913, with Lefty Tyler and Hub Perdue each notching 16 wins and Dick Rudolph winning 14 games.

The team was strengthened for the 1914 season by the addition of Johnny Evers, who'd been the Chicago Cubs' second baseman for twelve years (as part of the "Tinker-

1913 Wellesley College baseball team. The "regulation sport costume" was specified by the Rules and Regulations of the Athletic Department: blue bloomers, white middy blouse worn with a black tie, black shoes and stockings, black hair ribbon. The "W" that some of the players are wearing was awarded based on health ("including posture"), discipline, and technical skill. Infringency of training rules debarred a team member from wearing a "W." The training rules included:

A. Retire at 10 P.M. and not rise before 6:30 A.M.

B. Take a cold bath or plunge every morning. In special cases permission may be obtained from the Head of the Sport for the substitution of tepid bath or dry rub.

C. Eat nothing between meals, except fresh fruit. (Apples, pears, grapes, oranges, grape-fruit.)

D. Refrain absolutely from eating candy, coffee and tea.

E. Eat three regular meals each day (at morning, noon, and night).

F. Rest undisturbed for one consecutive quarter hour (at least) every afternoon.

Wellesley baseball began as a recreational activity in 1897. The sport became an official part of the physical education program in 1911. *Photo courtesy of Wellesley College Archives.*

This commemorative poster is a souvenir from "Maranville Day" in 1913. Rabbit Maranville had come up to the Boston Braves from the New Bedford Whalers at the end of the 1912 season. The following year, he was such a sensation that a Day was given in his honor. On July 19, 1913, two thousand supporters from his home town of Springfield, Massachusetts, as well as the mayors of Springfield and Boston were in attendance. The *Boston Herald* reported the next day: "Just how strongly Walter J. Maranville, the diminutive shortstop of the Boston Braves, has endeared himself to the hearts of baseball fans in this section was shown yesterday afternoon when 15,000 persons jammed their way into the small space at the South End Park to pay homage to the 'Rabbit.' Not only was the little fellow, whose game is causing him to be the most-talked-of player in the National League, showered with gifts, but he, with his team-mates, crowned the festivities by squeezing through a 5 to 4 victory over the Cubs." Among the gifts presented to "the little fellow" were a horseshoe of flowers (pictured), a silver loving cup, a watch and chain, a diamond stickpin, and "a 25 cent can of salmon." *Photo courtesy of the Boston Public Library, Print Department.*

The 1914 Providence Grays. The big fellow in the middle of the back row is Babe Ruth. In his major-league debut with the Boston Red Sox, on July 11 of 1914, Ruth pitched against Cleveland, getting credit for the win when Duffy Lewis pinch hit for him and scored the winning run. After two games with the Sox, Ruth was sent to Providence. In six weeks with the club, he won 9 of 11 decisions, helping pitch the Grays to the International League championship. He returned to Boston for the rest of the season, beating the New York Yankees in the first game after his return. *Photo courtesy of Barry Halper.*

to-Evers-to-Chance doubleplay combination). Although some baseball men thought Evers was far past his prime, Gaffney spent $25,000 to acquire the veteran.

Despite the addition of Evers, there was little hope that the 1914 squad would do much better than the line-up of the year before. Stallings himself described the roster as "one .300 hitter [Joe Connolly], the worst outfield that ever flirted with sudden death, three pitchers [James, Rudolph, and Tyler], and a good working combination around second base [Evers and Maranville]." What Stallings called "the worst outfield" was so bad that he used two completely different sets of outfielders depending on whether the opposing pitcher was left-handed or right-handed (one of the earliest examples of platooning).

At first, predictions of a mediocre season appeared to be overly optimistic. The Braves settled into the National League cellar, a position they occupied as late as July 17. Then "The Miracle" began to unfold. The team started winning—and couldn't seem to lose. During one stretch in August, James, Rudolph, and Tyler won 20 straight games between them. They were caught by Hank Gowdy, an excellent defensive backstop, who was playing his first full season.

On August 23, the Braves moved into a first-place tie with the defending champion New York Giants. The two teams battled for the top spot over two weeks, until a critical Labor Day doubleheader in Boston.

Above: The "Miracle Man" of 1914, manager George Stallings. Stallings is seated with second baseman Johnny Evers. *Photo courtesy of Dennis Goldstein. Below:* Appearing among his three star pitchers—Dick Rudolph, Lefty Tyler, and Bill James (left to right). *Photo courtesy of Culver Pictures.*

Sept. 7, 1914: World Record Crowd of 75,000

On July 17, 1914, the Boston Braves were in last place in the National League with a record of 35 wins and 43 losses. Just over a month later, on August 23, the Braves moved into a first-place tie with the New York Giants, and for the next two weeks the teams kept trading the number one and two spots in the standings. On Labor Day, September 7, the teams were again deadlocked at 67–52. With a holiday doubleheader scheduled, the Braves were given permission from the Red Sox to play at Fenway Park, which could accommodate more spectators than the rickety old South End Grounds. As the *Boston Herald* reported the next day, not even Fenway could hold all the fans who wanted to see the games:

75, 000 PERSONS SEE BRAVES AND GIANTS DIVIDE
Teams Establish World Record in Playing Before More People at Two Games Than Ever Turned Out in Single Day in Entire History of Professional Baseball.
BOSTONS WIN 5 TO 4 AND THEN LOSE BY 10 TO 1
By Walter E. Hapgood

The Braves failed to get better than an even break against the Giants in their holiday games at Fenway Park, yesterday, but they did establish a world's record in playing before more people at the two games than ever before turned out in a single day—holiday or otherwise—in the entire history of professional baseball.

Conservative estimates, placed upon the paid attendance as closely as it was possible to figure it last night, made the size of the crowd at the morning game 35,000 while in the afternoon fully 40,000 fans fought their way into the grounds. Both in the morning and afternoon the selling of tickets at all of the gates had to be stopped and, in addition to the 75,000 who did succeed in getting inside, there were probably 25,000 more who made the trip to Fenway Park but in vain, being absolutely unable to gain admission. Fully 10,000 were turned away in the morning and there were at least 15,000 who fared a similar fate in the afternoon. It was altogether the greatest tribute to baseball—and to the Braves—that this city has ever witnessed.

The morning game went to Stallings' men, 5 to 4, putting Boston into the lead once again in the National League race with a margin of one full game over the Giants. The Braves, however, maintained that advantage only for a few hours and when the second game was over the Giants had managed to get back what they had lost in the morning, the standing once more reverting to an even-up tie between Boston and New York.

Boston's victory in the morning was a distinctly Braves' performance, Stallings' men coming from the rear when more than one-half of the fans were resigned to defeat. The Braves went into the last half of the ninth inning one run behind, but after one man had been retired Boston very hurriedly batted two men around on clean hitting and, amid the repetition of world's series scenes, Boston had pulled the game out of the fire. The big crowd, unaccustomed to seeing the Braves perform in that fashion, fairly went wild with joy while Christy Mathewson, who had been trying to check Boston's onward march, walked back to the New York dug-out disheartened and discouraged. After pitching masterly baseball all the way through, Messrs. Devore, Moran and Evers had lodged hits at the critical moment against him and switched a defeat into a victory.

It was a great game, and a greater finish.

BOSTON	ab.	r.	bh.	tb.	po.	a.	e.
Moran, cf	5	2	3	4	3	0	0
Evers, 2b	5	0	1	1	4	1	0
Connolly, lf	4	1	3	5	2	0	0
Gilbert, rf	4	0	0	0	0	0	0
Mann, rf	0	0	0	0	0	0	0
Schmidt, 1b	4	1	2	3	9	1	0
Smith, 3b	4	0	2	3	2	4	1
Maranville, ss	3	0	0	0	3	3	0
Gowdy, c	4	0	0	0	4	2	0
Rudolph, p	3	0	0	0	0	1	0
★ Devore	1	1	1	1	0	0	0
Totals	37	5	12	17	27	12	1

NEW YORK	ab.	r.	bh.	tb.	po.	a.	e.
Snodgrass, cf	4	1	1	2	2	1	0
Doyle, 2b	4	0	2	2	0	6	0
Burns, lf	4	0	2	2	3	0	0
Fletcher, ss	4	1	2	3	2	3	1
Robertson, rf	2	0	0	0	0	0	0
Murray, rf	1	0	0	0	1	0	0
Grant, 3b	4	1	1	1	1	0	0
Merkle, 1b	4	0	0	0	10	0	0
McLean, c	4	1	2	2	6	0	0
Mathewson, p	3	0	1	2	0	2	0
Totals	34	4	11	14	25	12	1

★ *Batted for Rudolph in ninth inning.*

Innings	1	2	3	4	5	6	7	8	9		
Boston	1	0	0	1	0	0	0	1	2	—	5
New York	0	1	0	0	3	0	0	0	0	—	4

Two-base hits—Moran, Connolly 2, Schmidt, Smith, Fletcher, Snodgrass, Mathewson. Sacrifice hit—Robertson. Stolen base—McLean. First base on balls—Maranville. First base on errors—New York 1, Boston 1. Left on bases—Boston 8, New York 4. Struck out—Gilbert 2, Schmidt, Gowdy, Rudolph, Doyle, Merkle 3. Double plays—Smith to Schmidt; Rudolph to Schmidt to Smith; Maranville to Evers to Schmidt. Time—2h. Umpires—Klem and Emslie. Attendance—35,000.

The next day, in the third and final game of the series, Boston defeated New York 8–3 to take sole possession of first place. For the remainder of the season, and in the World Series, the Braves played their home games in Fenway Park.

At the time of the Labor Day doubleheader in Boston, the war in Europe was one month old, but not yet attracting great attention in the United States, which had declared its neutrality. Within a few years, two of the men who played in the September 7 games would become known for their roles in the conflict: Braves catcher Hank Gowdy would be the first of 227 baseball players to enlist for combat, and Giants third baseman Eddie Grant would be the first of three major leaguers to be killed in action.

Boston baseball fans were feverish with excitement over the Braves' turnabout, and had been packing South End Grounds to the bursting point. Starting with the Labor Day doubleheader against the Giants, the Braves played the rest of their home games in the Red Sox' larger Fenway Park.

After the series with the Giants in Boston, the Braves maintained sole possession of first place. In the last month of the season, the "Miracle Braves" continued to win games at an incredible pace, taking 25 of their last 31, to finish the season 10 1/2 games over New York.

Bill James, who had won only six games in his rookie season the year before, led the league in winning percentage with a 26–7 mark. Dick Rudolph also won 26 games, against 10 losses. Lefty Tyler matched his 1913 mark by notching 16 wins.

Johnny Evers and Rabbit Maranville anchored the team's defense, and performed so well that they finished first and second respectively in the balloting for league MVP (the Braves took the top three spots, as pitcher Bill James finished third in the voting).

Having captured the National League pennant, it looked as if the miracle was about to end. The Braves' opponents in the World Series were the Philadelphia Athletics, managed by Connie Mack. The Athletics were the defending World's Champions and had won the World Series in three of the past four years. Mack's team was one of the best in baseball history, boasting the "$100,000 infield" of Stuffy McInnis, Eddie Collins, Jack Barry, and Home Run Baker, and featuring three future Hall-of-Famers—Chief Bender, Herb Pennock, and Eddie Plank—on its pitching staff.

The first two games of the Series were played in Philadelphia. Boston shocked Bender and the Athletics by taking the opener 7–1, with Dick Rudolph getting the win. The second game was a pitching duel between Bill James and Eddie Plank, which the Braves won 1–0 with a run in the ninth inning.

Games Three and Four were played in Boston, in Fenway Park. The third game of the series was a thrilling extra-inning affair. The score was tied 2–2 after nine. In the tenth, the Athletics went ahead 4–2, but the Braves came back to tie it again in the bottom of the inning with the help of a Hank Gowdy home run. Bill James relieved Lefty Tyler in the eleventh and shut down the Athletics for two innings, until Boston won the game with a run in the bottom of the twelfth. Dick Rudolph took the mound again in Game Four and defeated Philadelphia 3–1 to give the Braves the World's Championship. It was the first sweep in modern World Series history, and "The Miracle" was complete.

Dick Rudolph and Bill James each won two games in the series, and Hank Gowdy and Johnny Evers were the batting heroes with .545 and .438 averages, respectively.

Oct. 12, 1914, prior to Boston's first home game of the World Series. The Braves had taken the first two games of the series in Philadelphia, and were on their way to sweeping the Athletics in four straight. The two men in Indian garb (who look like they're probably natives of Dorchester) have *OH YOU BRAVES* on their headbands. The man in the top hat is Mayor "Honey Fitz" Fitzgerald, proudly wearing his Boston Royal Rooters badge. The player in the center is Braves catcher Hank Gowdy, who led the team's hitting attack during the series, posting a batting average of .545. Next to Gowdy, wearing a dark bowler and sporting a flower in his lapel, is Braves owner James Gaffney. To the right, a couple more of the Royal Rooters fill out the gathering of Boston well-wishers. *Photo courtesy of the Library of Congress.*

Connie Mack was so humiliated at the loss that he sold most of his Athletics players during the off season.

Braves owner James Gaffney was certain that the good times would last and that a larger ballpark was necessary to fit all the spectators who would come to see his team play. On March 20, 1915, ground was broken on the site of the old Allston Golf Links for a new park which Gaffney promised would be "the world's largest ballpark ever." He delivered on his promise, building baseball's first million-dollar facility (but maintaining some tradition by replanting the infield grass from South End Grounds in the new park). On August 18, 1915, Braves Field opened with 43,500 fans in attendance—the largest crowd ever to witness a baseball game anywhere. Shortly after it opened, writer F. C. Lane described the park in *Baseball Magazine*: "The field at Boston is vast, simple in its line, Grecian in its architecture. There is something wonderfully imposing in the huge field, the stupendous sweep of the grandstand, and yet in all its multiform complexity, there is a quiet, harmonious unity. It seems as though an old Greek amphitheatre had been torn bodily from the Attic hills in the days when Athens ruled the world and had been transported to the low knolls and rolling valleys of the environs of Boston."

Unfortunately, it would be a while until the Braves would play a World Series game in their new home. Boston's National Leaguers finished in second place in 1915, dropped to third the next year, then fell to sixth place in 1917 and seventh in 1918. Braves Field was the site of World Series games in 1915 and 1916, but the team playing in them was the Red Sox, who were allowed to use the new grounds as repayment for the Braves having used Fenway Park in 1914. The Braves wouldn't make it into another World Series until 1948.

PORTLAND DUFFS

Maine was without an organized baseball franchise for several years until Portland rejoined the New England League in 1913. The team was owned and managed by Hugh Duffy, the "Heavenly Twin" of the Boston Beaneaters who had set the major-league single season batting mark with a .440 average in 1894.

Duffy, a native of Cranston, Rhode Island, had himself played in the New England League in 1887, before launching a major-league career that would land him in the Baseball Hall of Fame. Just as the Boston Red Sox were once called the "Somersets" after their owner Charles Somers, and the Braves were known as the "Doves" because of the Dovey brothers, the Portland club was also nicknamed for its owner-manager: the "Duffs."

The home opener for the Duffs was on May 8, when 9,000 fans crowded into Portland's brand-new Bayside Park to cheer the return of professional baseball to the city.

Of the eight teams in the 1913 New England League, all but Portland were from Massachusetts. The Duffs remained in contention throughout the season and finished in second place behind the Lowell Grays.

A second Maine club, the Lewiston Cupids ("Cupid" was the nickname of team owner Joseph W. Burns), joined the New England League in 1914, but neither Portland nor Lewiston made much of a run for the pennant, which was won by the Lawrence Pirates of Massachusetts.

In 1915, the Portland Duffs finally broke the Bay State's stranglehold on the league title. After a season-long battle with Lawrence for the top spot, Portland clinched the championship with a 3–2 defeat of the Lewiston Cupids in Bayside Park on August 31.

The next year, Portland entered the new Eastern League (made up entirely of New England cities, and no relation to the Eastern League that began in the nineteenth century). The Duffs again battled throughout the year, barely losing out at the end of the season to the New London Millionaires of Connecticut.

Hugh Duffy left Portland after the 1916 season to become baseball coach at Harvard University. He sold the team to showman Hiram Abrams, who was more interested in spectacle than baseball. For opening day (called "Getaway Day") in 1917, Abrams staged elaborate festivities that included movie stars Fatty Arbuckle and Norma Talmadge and

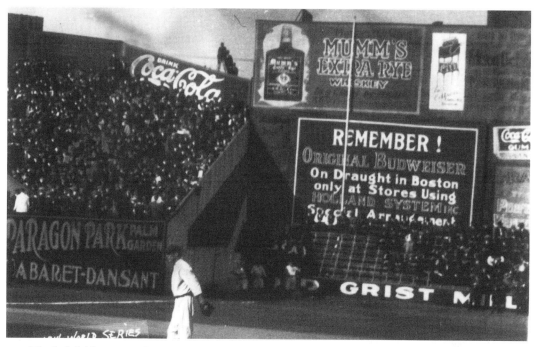

The left field corner of Fenway Park during the 1914 World Series. The Boston Red Sox permitted the Braves to use the park for home games to accomodate larger crowds. As can be seen in the photograph, the Braves further increased seating capacity by erecting wooden bleachers on Duffy's Cliff, the same area where the Royal Rooters had battled police two years earlier. *Photo courtesy of Michael Gershman.*

motion picture executives Jesse Lasky, Marcus Loew, and Adolph Zukor. The headline in the next day's *Daily Eastern Argus* read "5,000 See Movie Stars and Go Away Happy." Not mentioned in the headline was the fact that Portland lost the ballgame. With Duffy gone, the team needed a new name, and because of Abrams's fondness for movie people, the club was sometimes called the Portland Movies. Eventually, as the team sunk toward the bottom of the standings, not even spectacle could keep fans coming to the park. After the 1917 season, the franchise moved to Providence, Rhode Island.

As for Hugh Duffy, he later returned to the big leagues, managing the Boston Red Sox in 1921 and 1922. He remained on the Boston coaching staff for decades. In 1939, Duffy, who had won the batting Triple Crown in 1894, coached Red Sox rookie Ted Williams, who went on to win Triple Crowns in 1942 and 1947. Duffy was still an active Red Sox scout when he died at age 87 in 1954.

THREE CHAMPIONSHIPS
While the Miracle Braves were capturing most of the attention of Boston baseball fans in 1914, the Red Sox were also on their way to a resurgence. The Sox were Philadelphia's only competition for the American League pennant and ended the season in second place, a strong rebound from their fourth-place finish the year before.

Several important new faces appeared in the Red Sox lineup in 1914. One was

Lizzie Murphy, of Warren, Rhode Island, was billed as the "Queen of Baseball" during her long barnstorming career. By age fifteen, she was playing for local amateur teams. Within five years, she was established as a professional baseball player (the 1913 Warren directory gives her occupation as "ball player"). After a few years of semi-pro ball in Warren, Murphy was signed by the Providence Independants and barnstormed with them throughout New England. In 1918, she joined Ed Carr's Boston All-Stars, a semi-pro barnstorming team that included several former major leaguers. She remained with the All-Stars for 17 years, playing over 100 games a season. Between innings, Murphy supplemented her salary by selling autographed copies of this photograph to spectators. *Photo courtesy of the National Baseball Library & Archive, Cooperstown, N.Y.*

rookie Everett "Deacon" Scott, who made his major-league debut on April 14 and would be the team's regular shortstop for eight years; he would go on to set a record (later broken by Lou Gehrig) of playing in 1,307 consecutive games. Another was big Ernie Shore, who posted a 10–5 pitching record in his first season with the Sox and became one of the club's most dependable pitchers. Finally, there was left-handed pitcher Babe Ruth, who earned a win in his first major-league appearance on July 11; he was sent back to the minors, but returned at the end of the season, finishing the year with a record of 2–1.

Other young players, especially the pitchers, continued to develop. Rube Foster, who had been 3–4 in his rookie season of 1913, improved to win 14 games. Spitball pitcher Dutch Leonard, who had won 14 games as a rookie in 1913, notched 19 wins with only 5 defeats; he also set a twentieth century record for lowest earned run average with a 0.96 mark (a record which still stands). For the veteran pitchers, results were mixed: Ray Collins led the team in victories with his second straight 20-win season, but Smokey Joe Wood (who was suffering from arm trouble) and Hugh Bedient only posted 9 and 8 wins, respectively.

The "Golden Outfield" of Speaker, Hooper, and Lewis continued to play exceptional ball, as did third baseman Larry Gardner. Bill Carrigan was in his first full season as Red Sox manager and worked behind the plate in most of the team's games.

In 1915, it all came together for the Red Sox, as the team won 101 games to beat out the Detroit Tigers for the pennant.

The American League's top four pitchers in winning percentage were all on the Red Sox staff: Smokey Joe Wood led with a 15–5 record (sadly, he would never win another game—but he successfully switched to the outfield where he continued playing until 1922); Ernie Shore and Rube Foster had identical records of 19–8; and, in his first full season, Babe Ruth posted a 18–8 mark. Dutch Leonard, at 15–7, wasn't far behind the others. Rookie Carl Mays, a submarine style pitcher with a reputation for throwing at batters (in 1920, Mays would kill Cleveland shortstop Ray Chapman with a pitch), made his debut with the Sox on April 15; he led the league in saves with 7, and picked up 6 wins.

Although it didn't attract great notice at the time, on May 6 of 1915, Babe Ruth hit his first major-league home run off Yankee pitcher Jack Warhop. Ruth was used solely as a pitcher (and would be until 1918), but his bat was already a valuable part of Boston's offensive arsenal. He would hit .315 on the year with a slugging average of .576.

The Red Sox then faced the Philadelphia Phillies in the World Series. After losing the opener in Philadelphia, Boston went on to win four close games in a row to take the World's Championship.

Tris Speaker was no longer with Boston in 1916, and the team's offense suffered from the loss. Larry Gardner, who batted .308, was the only .300 hitter on the club. Strong pitching carried the Sox to another pennant, however.

Babe Ruth was Boston's top pitcher in 1916. He won 23 games and led the American League with a 1.75 earned run average. On August 15, in Fenway Park, Ruth hooked up with Walter Johnson in one of baseball's greatest pitching duels; the two men hurled shutouts against each other until the Red Sox scored in the thirteenth inning to give Ruth a 1–0 win.

The ticket booth of Braves Field. Opened in 1915, the park was the site of a World Series that fall, with the Red Sox using it as their home grounds. The Boston Braves didn't play a World Series in the park until 1948, and their final game in Braves Field was played on September 21, 1952. The structure shown here now houses the Boston University Police Station. *Photo courtesy of Michael Gershman.*

Boston's World Series opponents in 1916 were the Brooklyn Dodgers (then called the "Robins" after manager Wilbert Robinson). Boston won the opener at home (in Braves Field) behind the pitching of Ernie Shore and Carl Mays. The second game, also in Braves Field, matched Babe Ruth against the Dodgers' Sherry Smith. Ruth gave up an inside-the-park home run in the first inning, but in the third he drove in a run to tie the game. Both pitchers then threw shutout ball until the Red Sox scored the winning run in the bottom of the fourteenth inning. Boston went on to win its second straight World's Championship four games to one.

In December 1916, New York theatrical producer Harry Frazee gained control of the Red Sox. And Boston still hasn't recovered from the effects.

Bill Carrigan retired after the 1916 season and second baseman Jack Barry replaced him as the team's manager for 1917. Although the pitching was still strong—Ruth won 24 games and Mays 22—the hitting was too weak for the Red Sox to repeat. The club finished in second place, nine games behind the pennant-winning White Sox.

With the country now fighting in "The Great War," 1918 was to be one of the most unusual seasons in baseball history. At the same time that they were requiring players to engage in pre-game military drills (often using bats as rifles), baseball owners were trying to get ballplayers exempted from the draft. The Secretary of War rejected the owners' arguments, and the regular season ended a month early, on September first.

June 23, 1917: Greatest Battle Ever Twirled At Fenway Park

Boston Red Sox pitcher Ernie Shore achieved one of baseball's greatest feats in history's most unusual relief appearance. The big right-hander was Boston's fourth starter, behind Babe Ruth, Carl Mays, and Dutch Leonard. Shore was sitting on the bench when starting pitcher Ruth walked the first Washington player to face him on four straight pitches. After Ruth got himself ejected for arguing the calls (and subsequently punched the umpire), Shore was called in and allowed eight warm-up throws before taking the Babe's place. The runner on first was thrown out attempting to steal second, and Shore retired the next 26 batters in a row. The next day's *Boston Post* described his perfect performance:

Shore Pitches Record Game After Ruth is Canned for Hitting Umpire

If Shore won a no-hit victory over the Senators, Babe Ruth, one of the greatest assets in the Red Sox pitching corps, likewise accomplished a no hit performance over Brick Owens, for, at the very start of the double matinee, he committed an assault upon that official which is likely to cost himself and the Boston club pretty dearly. No matter how much the umpire may have been wrong in his judgment, there can be little justification for Ruth's act, a demonstration which has never before been made by a Red Sox player in this city.

Morgan was the first of the Washington men to bat, and after he had been awarded first base Ruth lost his temper and asked Owens to keep his eyes open.

"You get back there and pitch or I'll run you out of the ball park," the arbiter threatened.

"If you run me out of the ball park I'll take a punch at you on my way," the angry player retorted.

"You're out now," yelled Owens, waving his arm in a gesture of banishment.

Ruth lost his head completely and rushed for the umpire. Catcher Thomas sprang in front of the big pitcher and as Ruth swung at the umpire's head, Thomas apparently deflected the blow. Before Babe could reach the umpire again not only Thomas but Barry himself had gotten in the way and the result was that Babe was exiled without any further collision between himself and the umps. The Boston club will wait anxiously to see what punishment Ban Johnson may mete out.

According to the umpire, Ruth did succeed in hitting him although he admits it was a light, glancing blow on the cheek, but Manager Barry, Heinie Wagner and others of the Boston team insist that Thomas warded off the blow and on that account they are hoping that Babe will be mercifully dealt with.

Owens showed good judgment in making no effort to return the blow. His coolness probably prevented further trouble, although the police were promptly on the spot.

It is rather unfortunate that this incident in a way dimmed the magnificent performance of Shore. Taking Ruth's place with a brief warming up and handicapped by having a man on first base Shore proceeded to go through with a feat that will have the whole baseball world sitting up and taking notice.

Agnew, who caught a marvellous game and batted terrifically, caught Morgan when he tried to steal. Then Shore retired the next 26 men just as fast as they came to bat, three brilliant plays, one by Scott and two by Duffy Lewis, making the achievement possible.

As the game waned and it became apparent that Shore was on his way to a no-hit game the tension grew greater. In the eighth the fast fielding of Shore himself saved a hit, and in the ninth a wonderful catch by Lewis and a pretty play by Barry gave Ernie the credit of pitching the greatest battle ever twirled at Fenway Park.

Lewis' spectacular catch off Henry in the ninth and Barry's clever running catch of an attempted bunt by a pinch hitter finally clinched Shore's claim to take his place with the pitching immortals.

BOSTON	AB.	BH.	PO.	A.	WASHINGTON	AB.	BH.	PO.	A.
Hooper, rf	4	1	0	0	Morgan, 2b	2	0	5	2
Barry, 2b	4	0	2	1	E. Fos'r, 3b	3	0	1	3
Hob'zell, 1b	4	0	12	2	Leon'd, 3b	0	0	0	1
Gardn'r, 3b	4	1	2	1	Milan, cf	3	0	1	0
Lewis, lf	4	3	2	0	Rice, rf	3	0	3	0
Walker, cf	3	1	4	0	Gharrity, 1b	0	0	0	0
Scott, ss	3	0	1	5	Judge, 1b	3	0	10	1
Thomas, c	0	0	0	0	Jamie'n, lf	3	0	0	0
Agnew, c	3	3	2	1	Shanks, ss	3	0	1	2
Ruth, p	0	0	0	0	Henry, c	3	0	1	0
Shore, p	2	0	2	6	Ayers, p	2	0	2	8
Totals	31	9	27	16	*Menosky	1	0	0	0
					Totals	26	0	24	17

* Hit for Ayers in 9th.

Innings	1	2	3	4	5	6	7	8	9		
Boston	0	1	0	0	0	0	3	0		—	4

Runs—Gardner, Walker, Agnew, Shore. *Errors*—Foster 2, Rice. *Two-base hit*—Walker, Agnew. *Sacrifice hits*—Walker, Shore, Scott. *Base on balls*—Off Ruth 1. *Struck out*—By Shore 2. *Double plays*—Ayers to Foster to Judge, Ayers to Judge. *Time*—1h, 45m. *Umpires*—McCormick and Owens.

Ban Johnson, usually a stern disciplinarian, gave Ruth a light penalty: a 10-day suspension and a fine of $100. Johnson explained that his leniency was because the Red Sox were in a tight pennant race with Chicago. When Ruth returned to the line-up, he lost his first two starts, and the White Sox went on to win the championship. As for Ernie Shore, he ended the season with 13 victories, and would win only 7 more games in the major leagues. Some baseball purists still argue whether Shore should be credited with a perfect game for his relief appearance because he faced only 26 batters.

Rosters were unstable as regular players left to enlist for military service or to take jobs in the defense industries, and a succession of mediocre replacements substituted for them on the ballfield. Red Sox players Jack Barry, Dutch Leonard, Duffy Lewis, and Herb Pennock all were lost for part of the season to the armed services.

Boston filled gaps in its roster by picking up some of the veterans that Connie Mack was continuing to sell off: first baseman Stuffy McInnis, pitcher Bullet Joe Bush, center fielder Amos Strunk, and catcher Wally Schang. The club also acquired a couple of older journeymen (both were 35 and unlikely to be drafted): second baseman Dave Shean and left fielder George Whiteman, who had appeared in four games with the 1907 Red Sox (Whiteman later set the record for most minor league games played with 3282, accumulating 3388 base hits from 1905 to 1929).

Several factors contributed to Babe Ruth's shift to the outfield in 1918. One was that his bat was such an obvious asset to the line-up and a great fan attraction. Another was that Sad Sam Jones filled in admirably for Ruth in the pitching rotation when the Babe missed a few starts in May due to a cold. Finally, George Whiteman was such a defensive disaster in left field, that Ruth was sent out to take his place. After playing 59 games in the outfield, Ruth later returned to the pitching rotation, winning 9 of his final 11 decisions.

Playing a 126-game season under new manager Ed Barrow (Harry Hooper actually made most of the decisions involving game strategy), Boston eked out another American League pennant in 1918, finishing 2 1/2 games ahead of Cleveland. Sam Jones, who had been 0–2 for the Red Sox over the past two seasons, blossomed into a superb pitcher while filling in for Ruth, winning 16 games against only 5 losses to lead the American League in winning percentage. Babe Ruth, meanwhile, led the league in slugging average and tied for the lead in home runs.

The Red Sox' opponents in the World Series were the Chicago Cubs, who had run away with the National League title. The Cubs so feared Ruth's bat, that they played their home games of the Series in Comiskey Park because it had a deeper right field than Cubs Park (later to be called Wrigley Field).

In the opener, though, it was Ruth's pitching that did in Chicago, as he won a 1–0 shutout over Hippo Vaughn. The teams split the next two games. Ruth won again in the fourth contest, but he was finally scored on after pitching 29 2/3 consecutive innings of shutout ball in World Series games (a record that would stand until Whitey Ford broke it in 1961).

The pitching staff that led the Boston Red Sox to three World's Championships from 1915 to 1918: Rube Foster, Carl Mays, Ernie Shore, Babe Ruth, Dutch Leonard (left to right). *Photo courtesy of Culver Pictures.*

Game Five in Boston was delayed by a brief players' strike. The three-man National Commission had unilaterally decided to reduce the percentage of the gate receipts that would be allocated to the players. The players sought a meeting with the Commission members (Ban Johnson, August Herrmann, and National League president John Heydler) to discuss the new arrangements, but the Commission instead elected to spend the morning of the fifth game in the bar of the Copley Plaza Hotel. The players refused to dress for the game. Johnson, Herrmann, and Heydler finally showed up at the ballpark and met with player representatives. The players agreed to go ahead with the game when they realized that the members of the National Commission were by now too drunk to discuss the matter anyway. The game started an hour late, and Boston was shut out.

The next day, Carl Mays won Game Six by a score of 2-1. The Red Sox had won another World Series, their fifth in five Series appearances.

Because of the attempted strike, the National Commission withheld the World Series emblems (usually a commemorative watch, stick pin, or watch fob) that should have been awarded to the Red Sox players. Despite decades of efforts, the emblems still haven't been issued—and Boston has never won another World Series.

Pressed for money to finance his Broadway productions, Harry Frazee began to dismantle the Red Sox roster. From 1919 to 1923, Babe Ruth, Carl Mays, Ernie

Shore, Duffy Lewis, Herb Pennock, Everett Scott, Wally Schang, and Joe Bush were all sent to the Yankees. When Babe Ruth was sold, irate Bostonians began putting "For Sale" signs on public landmarks throughout the city.

When Frazee gave up ownership of the team in 1923, he was not missed by local baseball fans. As Babe Ruth himself said, "They'll never build any monuments to Harry Frazee in Boston."

The Red Sox finally rebuilt in the 1940s, and fielded some excellent teams in later decades, but so far another World's Championship eludes the club. As the notion of a curse on the team began to take hold, numerous proposals to lift the evil spell have been put forth. They range from the symbolic (issue the 1918 World Series emblems) to the obvious (acquire an effective bullpen) to the bizarre: former Red Sox pitcher Bill "Spaceman" Lee suggested disinterring Babe Ruth's remains and bringing them to Fenway Park where The Bambino would be given a public apology for selling him to the Yankees.

Even if "The Curse" is a myth, the frustration experienced by New England baseball fans is all too real. For many of them, the 1918 World Series marked the end of an era. And for some, time has stood still thereafter. In April of 1995, Boston Mayor Tom Menino proposed that the city adopt as its slogan: "Boston: Home of the 1918 World Champion Red Sox."

BIBLIOGRAPHY

BOOKS

Alexander, Charles. *Our Game.* New York: Henry Holt, 1991.

Allen, Lee, and Tom Meany. *Kings of the Diamond.* New York: Putnam, 1965.

Anderson, Will. *Was Baseball Really Invented in Maine?.* Portland, ME: Will Anderson, 1992.

Berlage, Gai. *Women in Baseball: The Forgotten History.* Westport, CT: Praeger, 1994.

Blanchard, John, editor, *The H Book of Harvard Athletics, 1852-1922.* Cambridge, MA: Harvard University Press, 1923.

Cappio, Alfred. *"Slide, Kelly, Slide": The Story of Michael J. Kelly.* Paterson, NJ: Passaic County Historical Society, 1962.

Catton, Bruce. *The Civil War.* New York: Fairfax Press, 1980.

Clark, Dick, and Larry Lester, editors. *The Negro Leagues Book.* Cleveland, OH: SABR, 1994.

Clifton, Merritt. *Disorganized Baseball, vol. II: Baseball in Vermont (1887-1935).* Monroe, CT: SAMISDAT, 1991.

Creamer, Robert. *Babe: The Legend Comes to Life.* New York: Simon and Schuster, 1974.

Davids, L. Robert, editor. *This Date in Baseball History.* Cooperstown, NY: SABR, 1976.

Ellard, Harry. *Base Ball in Cincinnati.* Cincinnati: Johnson & Hardin, 1907 (reprint, Ohio Book Store, 1987).

Gershman, Michael. *Diamonds: The Evolution of the Ballpark.* New York: Houghton Mifflin, 1993.

Goldstein, Warren. *Playing for Keeps: A History of Early Baseball.* Ithaca, NY: Cornell University Press, 1989.

Gregorich, Barbara. *Women at Play: The Story of Women in Baseball.* San Diego, CA: Harcourt Brace, 1993.

Honig, Donald. *Baseball: The Illustrated History of America's Game.* New York: Crown, 1990.

Hurd, Richard. *A History of Yale Athletics, 1840-1888.* New Haven, CT: R. M. Hurd, 1888.

Lansche, Jerry. *The Forgotten Championships: Postseason Baseball, 1882-1981.* Jefferson, NC: McFarland, 1989.

Levin, Leonard, editor. *Days of Greatness: Providence Baseball 1875-1885.* Cooperstown, NY: SABR, 1984.

Levine, Peter. *A. G. Spalding and the Rise of Baseball.* New York: Oxford University Press, 1985.

Lieb, Fred. *Connie Mack.* New York: Putnam, 1945.

————. *The Baseball Story.* New York: Putnam, 1950.

————. *Baseball As I Have Known It.* New York: Coward, McCann & Geoghegan, 1977.

Lowry, Philip. *Green Cathedrals.* Reading, MA: Addison–Wesley, 1992.

MacWilliams, Don. *Yours in Sport, vol. I: Baseball, Basketball, Boxing and Bowling in Maine.* Lewiston, ME: Monmouth Press, 1969.

Maranville, Walter. *Run, Rabbit, Run.* Cleveland, OH: SABR, 1991.

Morse, Jacob. *Sphere and Ash: History of Baseball.* Boston: Camden House, 1984 (c1888).

Murphy, J. M. *The National Pastime: Napoleon Lajoie.* Kansas City, MO: SABR, 1988.

Nemec, Raymond. *A Minor League Directory.* Downers Grove, IL: Raymond Nemec, 1971.

Okkonen, Marc. *The Federal League of 1914-1915.* Garrett Park, MD: SABR, 1989.

————. *Baseball Memories: 1900-1909.* New York: Sterling, 1992.

————. *Baseball Uniforms of the 20th Century.* New York: Sterling, 1993.

Okrent, Daniel, and Harris Lewine, editors. *The Ultimate Baseball Book.* Boston: Houghton Mifflin, 1988.

Peterson, Robert. *Only the Ball Was White.* New York: Oxford University Press, 1970.

Reichler, Joseph, editor. *The Baseball Encyclopedia.* Third Edition. New York: Macmillan, 1976.

Ritter, Lawrence. *The Glory of Their Times.* New York: Macmillan, 1966.

————. *Lost Ballparks.* New York: Viking, 1992.

Ryczek, William. *Blackguards and Red Stockings, A History of Baseball's National Association, 1871-1875.* Jefferson, NC: McFarland, 1992.

Scheinin, Richard. *Field of Screams.* New York: Norton, 1994.

Seymour, Harold. *Baseball, The Early Years.* New York: Oxford University Press, 1960.

————. *Baseball, The Golden Age.* New York: Oxford University Press, 1971.

————. *Baseball, The People's Game.* New York: Oxford University Press, 1990.

Smith, Robert. *Baseball.* New York: Simon and Schuster, 1947.

Spalding, A. G. *Base Ball, America's National Game.* New York: Halo Books, 1991 (c1911).

Thorn, John. *A Century of Baseball Lore.* New York: Hart, 1974.

Thorn, John, and Pete Palmer, editors. *Total Baseball,* Fourth Edition. New York: Viking, 1995.

Thorn, John, and Mark Rucker, Editors. *The National Pastime: Baseball in the Nineteenth Century.* Cooperstown, NY: SABR, 1984.

——————————————————————. *The National Pastime: Baseball in the Deadball Era.* Cooperstown, NY: SABR, 1986.

Tiemann, Robert L., and Mark Rucker, editors. *Nineteenth Century Stars.* Kansas City, MO: SABR, 1989.

Ward, Geoffrey, and Ken Burns. *Baseball: An Illustrated History.* New York: Knopf, 1994.

White, Sol. *Sol White's History of Colored Baseball.* Philadelphia: University of Nebraska Press, 1995 (c1907).

Wills, Bret, and Gwen Aldridge. *Baseball Archaeology.* San Francisco: Chronicle Books, 1993.

Zoss, Joel, and John Bowman. *Diamonds in the Rough: The Untold History of Baseball.* New York: Macmillan, 1989.

ARTICLES

Barry, Jay. "He Pitched Baseball's First 'Perfect Game'," *Brown Alumni Monthly* (October 1964), pp. 26–29.

Bergen, Phil. "Lovett of the Lowells," *National Pastime,* 16 (1996), pp. 62–66.

Bevis, Charles. "The 1901 Boston Americans," *National Pastime,* 10 (1990), pp. 27–32.

Brock, Darryl. "The Wright Way," *Sports Heritage* (March/April 1987), pp. 35–94.

Brock, Darryl. "Mark Twain and the Great Base Ball Match," *National Pastime,* 14 (1994), pp. 55–58.

Davids, L. Robert. "John (Bud) Fowler: 19th Century Black Baseball Pioneer." Unpublished paper.

Felber, Bill. "Genesis of a Miracle," *Sports History,* (January 1990), pp. 45-49.

Goslow, Charles. "Fairground Days: When Worcester was a National League City (1880-82)," *Historical Journal of Massachusetts,* (Summer 1991), pp. 133–154.

Hack, Richard. "Four Series Surprises," *Sports History,* (January 1989), pp. 40-53.

Hunsinger Jr., Lou. "George W. Stovey," *National Pastime,* 14 (1994), pp. 80–82.

Husman, John. "J. Lee Richmond's Remarkable 1879 Season," unpublished presentation at SABR annual convention, July 6, 1984.

Ivor-Campbell, Frederick. "Extraordinary 1884," *National Pastime,* 13 (1993), pp. 16–23.

Keith, Larry. "Not Every Bloomer Held a Girl," *Sports Illustrated* (Nov. 9, 1970), p. M3.

Kearney, Seamus. "The Brattleboro Islanders," *National Pastime,* 15 (1995), pp. 5–9.

Kearney, Seamus. "Bill Thompson, Pioneer," *National Pastime,* 16 (1996), pp. 67–68.

Kleinknecht, Merl. "Blacks in 19th Century Organized Baseball," *Baseball Research Journal* (1977), pp. 118–127.

Lane, F. C. "The World's Greatest Baseball Park," *Baseball Magazine,* (October 1915), pp. 29-108.

Luse, Vern. "The Evolution of Minor League Classifications," *Minor League History Journal* (1991), pp. 11–12.

Malloy, Jerry. "The Pittsburgh Keystones and the 1887 Colored League," in *Baseball in Pittsburgh* (Cleveland, OH: SABR, 1995), pp. 49-53.

Overfield, Joseph. "James 'Deacon' White," *Baseball Research Journal* (1975), pp. 1–11.

Price, Bill. "Braves Field," *Baseball Research Journal* (1978), pp. 1–6.

Rucker, Mark. "History of Baseball Through Photography, Part IV: Stereo Views," *The Vintage & Classic Baseball Collector,* (December 1995), pp. 18-19.

Sloate, Barry. "Rare & Historical Baseball Books," *The Vintage & Classic Baseball Collector,* (September 1995), pp. 6-13.

Stout, Glenn. "The Grand Exalted Ruler of Rooters' Row," *The Red Sox Fan News,* (August 1986), pp. 18-22.

Stout, Glenn. "The Last Champions," *New England Sport,* (Summer 1993), pp. 23-36.

Thompson, Dick. "Matty and his Fadeaway," *Baseball Research Journal* (1996), pp. 93–96.

Thornton, Carolyn. "First 'Baseman' Shone in Semipro Ball," *Providence Journal-Bulletin,* (March 1994), p. 22.

Voight, David. "The Boston Red Stockings: The Birth of Major League Baseball," *New England Quarterly,* (December 1970), pp. 531–549.

Wagner, William. "The Champions of Boston?," *Oldtyme Baseball News,* (Vol. 6, Issue 6), p. 20.

Waldbauer, Richard. "A Social History of the Providence Grays," unpublished presentation at SABR annual convention, July 6, 1984.

PERIODICALS

Adams Transcript, 1859
Amherst Express, 1859
Bangor Commercial, 1907
Boston Globe, 1878–1995
Boston Herald, 1858-1914
Boston Post, 1878–1917
Boston Transcript, 1880
Brattleboro Reformer, 1911
The Dartmouth, 1882
Hartford Courant, 1875
Manchester Union, 1904
Meriden Republican, 1884
New England Base Ballist, 1868
New Haven Register, 1912

New Haven Union, 1912
Pawtucket Times, 1896
Portland Eastern Argus, 1886
Providence Journal, 1868–1912
Springfield Union, 1895
Vermont Phoenix, 1911
Williams Quarterly, 1864
Worcester Gazette, 1880–1992

INDEX